I USED TO BE AN ILLEGAL:
My Love Letter to America

JG MONACO

DEDICATION

I dedicate this book to my children, Alyssa, Victor, and Franco, for giving me the inspiration to write this book.

To my parents, my father Jesus Sr., my stepmother Piri, my mother Silvia, and my dad Edgar, for being an example of hard work and success in the face of tremendous adversities. To my brothers, Gustavo and Guillermo, and my sisters, Maria Andreina, Maria Gabriela and Maria Alejandra, for the love and respect we have for each other. To the rest of my family, for the love and understanding that you have always given me.

CONTENTS

PART ONE

Prologue	2
Chapter One	4
Chapter Two	22
Chapter Three	32
Chapter Four	42
Love Letter To America	50

PART TWO

Chapter Five	53
Chapter Six	67
Chapter Seven	77
Chapter Eight	86

PART THREE

Chapter Nine	101
The Endless Soul Of Immigrants	115
Chapter Ten	116
Chapter Eleven	130
Closing Statement	145
Special Thanks	148

ACKNOWLEDGMENTS

This is a work of non-fiction. Some names and identifying details have been changed to protect the privacy of individuals. Although the author and publisher have made every effort to ensure that the information in this book was correct at press time, the author and publisher do not assume and hereby disclaim any liability to any party for any loss, damage, or disruption caused by errors or omissions, whether such errors or omissions result from negligence, accident, or any other cause.

The author further acknowledges the trademarked status and trademark owners of various products referenced in this work, which have been used without permission. The publication/use of these trademarks is not authorized, associated with, or sponsored by the trademark owners.

PART ONE

PROLOGUE

I still recall the sweaty palms and butterflies churning in my stomach as I applied for my first job. I was in desperate need of employment, yet uncertainty clouded my thoughts as I stared at the application. Conceding defeat, I looked around for help.

"Excuse me sir—what do I write here?"

"Are you a citizen?"

"Yes, I am a Venezuelan citizen."

The man just grinned at me. Several seconds ticked by.

"What about here? What should I write?"

"Well, what are you?"

I looked at the paper again before replying, as if the answer would suddenly appear there in the blank box.

"I don't think I am black. I'm pretty sure I'm Latino, but I think I am white too."

He shook his head and smiled. My answer seemed to amuse him, but he just nodded. "Sure…if that's what you think you are."The next few minutes went by in silence, until I once again found myself stymied by a question.

"Sorry," I said a bit sheepishly," but I don't have a social security number yet."

"That's okay," he replied. "I can take care of that."

And he did.

When some people hear this story, they react with horror—they can't comprehend how a citizen of the United States could knowingly assist with the commission of a crime. Yet there is another side to the story, another perspective that I want to share with you. It isn't the story of clandestine crimes, but of a scared kid looking to get started with his life. You see, that conversation took place my first time reading through a job application here in America. It was the first time I became aware that being a Venezuelan citizen meant nothing outside of Venezuelan borders; the first time I became aware of the color of my skin, and the first time I realized that I may have not had what I needed to start the new life I sought. I didn't know what was I missing—I just knew I didn't have it.

The years since that day have been kind to me, though the journey has been long. Looking back, I realize that America has been an essential part of my life, a once-foreign land developing into the central character in the tale of who I am. When I think of the United States, I can't help but personify the country. Yes, to me, America is a living, breathing entity—and this book is my love letter to her.

America, I want to tell you how I see you, and how you look from the eyes of a forever-grateful immigrant. This is a tribute to you. These are my reasons for becoming who I am.

CHAPTER ONE

"Safety and security don't just happen, they are the result of collective consensus and public investment. We owe our children, the most vulnerable citizens in our society, a life free of violence and fear."
— Former President of South Africa, Nelson Mandela.

Venezuela, my homeland, was once a refuge for many immigrants running from persecution and the tragedies of war, a prosperous and promising nation with the same freedoms and opportunities Americans have enjoyed for generations. Ironically, I found myself looking for those same treasures the morning I left her to come to the United States. Unfortunately for me, my freedoms were lost somewhere between a populist speech and a disappointed democracy. In Venezuela, the land that nurtured me as a child, the brave are those who remain, exercising their freedoms; they are students, journalists and main street individuals that have the courage to stand for justice and despise any kind of political discrimination and corruption.

For some, when thinking about Venezuela, the first thoughts that come to mind are oil and a land of beautiful women; for me, its not only that land of beautiful women, but also the green of the trees standing along the side of the streets of my neighborhood, the memory of my dad driving me to school every morning, the newspaper guy at the traffic light, the smell of pencils and bread from my book-bag, my school uniform, the faces of my friends, teachers, and most importantly, my family.

I come from a modest and hard working family. I never felt poor but at the same time, I never felt entitled, never believed I could ask for much. I remember my parents working diligently and, though they were loving, they were strict about home rules. There was no tolerance for wasting food, water, clothing, or even toys; no talking back when being spoken to, homework and schoolwork were always done before play time commenced, I was expected to always clean up after myself, display good manners, be polite and respectful—and worst of all, to meet curfew. For some reason, it always seemed like I was the first kid that had to go home, usually in the middle of the most exciting part of the afternoon game.

Some of my earliest memories in Venezuela come from the beautiful and beloved city of Valencia and my family there-my great aunt Aura (Mi Bibita) and my great uncle Sergio (Mi Congo). I remember playing with them more than I remember playing with my own mother. Mi Congo was my favorite playmate and companion; actually, I was his favorite walking partner and grocery shopping wing-boy. From going to the local market, to visiting his mother in the middle of the city, we would do it all together, walking, walking, and walking some more.

Mi Congo was one of those folkloric characters found in close-knit communities, a man who knew everyone by name, always ready with a smile as he walked about, his hat perched on his head and a newspaper tucked under his arm. He was never scared to respectfully pay compliments to a beautiful woman nor engage in a political discussion about current events. His love for life and his family was only matched by his passion for bullfighting, an expression of culture for some like him, and a growing feeling of disgust for a grotesque show of animal suffering and cruelty for many others. He would make me laugh every time he smoothed over a disagreement with Mi Bibita about a household issue with nothing but his good humor and a kiss for his beloved wife. He had sayings and phrases that I still remember, he showed me that with kindness, even the most unpleasant person in the world would show his soft side, and with politeness, there was no door that would remain closed forever. I can still remember the afternoon naps at his house, when I would fall asleep on his chest while he hummed the Venezuelan National Anthem.

Mi Bibita was the sweet and caring grandmother that everyone dreams of. As my grandmother's sister, she shared a lot in common with her. Their dedication to their children and grandchildren showed in their simple but meaningful actions. Her beatific smile with every hello and goodbye, her incredibly delicious food, her hugs and kisses were each an expression of her love. When I became a father myself, I learned how fortunate I'd been for having both her and my grandmother by my side throughout my childhood. Mi Bibita's hands were soft and small and I loved how she always walked slowly but with determination. She would do her chores while singing Isabel Pantoja songs, she loved anything and everything from Spain, wore long and colorful dresses and smelled like baby powder. I remember being fed, showered, and dressed by her. She would always tell me that I was an ADECO (a member of the Democratic Action Party) and she would always end my afternoons with a spoonful of honey and some drops of lime to keep the colds and flu away. She would get aggravated every time Mi Congo would take me for such long walks to the market, and to this date, she talks to me as if I were still the same little boy she used to care for. In some ways, she has never stopped caring for me. I can close my eyes and still see her smiling, sitting on a rocking chair and praying with a long and purple rosary in the afternoons.

Like any other child, schools were my second home. My Kindergarten school, La Asuncion, was a tall white house surrounded by a small white fence. I remember my teacher, Nelly, and the first time I enjoyed the attentions of a girl friend. I shared my food from my blue Super Man lunch-box, but only on the days when my mother packed something I didn't like. My only concern in those years was making sure I had the fastest shoes in my school—I was always one of the shortest boys in my class, so being fast was technically my only advantage.

I can also recall in detail my elementary school years at U.E Romulo Gallegos. I made friends that I still remember playing with, boys like Pedro Manuel and Darío. My days would start very early in the morning since I had to be at school by 7:00 am. While it was still dark outside, I took a shower and put my uniform on while my mother made arepas with butter and shredded llanero cheese. Arepas are part of the typical Venezuelan diet, similar to grits but a little more refined. You can mix it with water and make dough, which is then fried or baked and filled with whatever you want. Butter and llanero cheese were the most common fillings at our house, while ham, bacon, salami or eggs were only for special occasions or weekends. My mid-morning lunch was packed during my first years of elementary school, but around third grade, my parents decided to start giving me an allowance instead. It was just enough to buy one empanada and a juice. If I wanted something else— like candy—I had to skip either drinking or eating. Sometimes I would skip drinking or eating for couple of days just to have a slice of chocolate cake or churros on fridays.

My school day would end around 12:00 pm, and since both of my parents worked, I had the pleasure of having Mr. Hanz and his ancient station wagon taking me home. Mr. Hanz was as old as his car, although he was much quieter. He was skinny, with white hair and a yellow mustache from all the smoking he did—smoking that made him match his wagon, which was beige with a brown interior. I can still recall the strong smell of old leather, dust, and cigarettes mixed with the smell of my book bag and my sweaty friends. See, since not all the windows would go down, the doors were rusty and heavy, and the car had no A/C or exhaust, we would ask him to drive fast just so we would get some fresh air. Thinking back on it, I realize Mr. Hanz' wagon was just an insult to the environment, but the ride was slow and loud. I would get a concentrated dose of lung cancer, possible exposure to tetanus or the flu and an adrenaline rush every afternoon with Mr. Hanz' tranport LLC.

Once home, my babysitter Belkys would be waiting for me. She usually had a warm lunch on the table and a whole routine for the rest of the afternoon. Belkys was young, maybe in her early twenties, with long, curly black hair and dark skin. I'm not sure why, but I remember that her hands were always very well kept. She was a black belt in Karate and needless to say, she was a tough cookie. She never allowed me to leave anything behind on my plate and she always made me take a nap after lunch. I didn't argue.

Like most kids, one of my least favorite things to do was visit my pediatrician. It wasn't just the threat of getting shots, though, but because the wait was always so long. As a child I didn't care how good my doctor was, I just knew it was going to be a boring afternoon. Now, as a father of three, I can appreciate the value of a good pediatrician. Dr. Juana Lopez would hold me, tickle me, hug me and knew my entire family by name. Her office was cold and smelled like alcohol and iodine, but she was and still is a very compassionate and dedicated Doctor.

I was a typical child with a typical childhood. I spent a lot of time playing with cars or toy cowboys, Indians, or soldiers. They were my favorite toys and I would spend hours playing if left alone. I didn't have much interest in TV until later, but I still remember getting my Atari when everyone else was getting their Nintendo—and I got my Nintendo when everyone else started playing with their new computers.

That was the story of my life; never poor, never rich, just enough to make me appreciate and enjoy everything my parents were able to provide. I grew up loving baseball, along with Christmas, Holy Week, and Carnivals. I am Magallanero (a fan of my home state's baseball team), my basketball team is Trotamundos, but above all, I am Vinotinto —a fan of any Venezuelan national team.

Before I turned four, my sister Andreina arrived. She was followed by another new addition, Gabriela, prior to my ninth birthday. Barely a year later, my third sister Alejandra came along. By October 1992, my mother had a ten year old son, a daughter who was six, a one year old baby girl and a newborn. The expansion of our family forced my parents to think about moving to Maracay, a neighboring city about an hour away. With most of my maternal family there, my mother felt she could find the support she needed while also helping with my grandparent's home, which seemed almost too big for them to maintain. So, we moved to my grandparent's house, a five bedroom home near the mountains of El Castaño.

My maternal grandfather, Modesto, was a hard-working man in love with cultivating the land. He tried his best to raise a respectful family. He would teach me about nature, the importance of simple acts such as planting a tree, how to make the best fertilizer and to enjoy the beauty of wild animals. Despite these cherished moments, Modesto possessed a very strict disposition. I'm still not certain if this sprang from the wisdom that develops with age, my selfishness as a child or if, over time, my own life experiences have revealed the possibility that his toughness was an attempt at hiding a sensitive side. Whatever the reason, the precious time with him ensured my Abuelo will always have a unique place in my childhood memories.

During those years when we lived with my grandparents, I grew especially close to my grandmother. Modesto's wife, Socorro, was perhaps the most caring and giving woman I have known apart from my own mother. She embodied love and dedication. I had the good fortune of living with her for several years. The smell of coffee in the mornings would blend with the aroma of homemade breakfast. My little sisters would look down through a window that overlooked my grandma's kitchen and ask if food was ready. My Abuela would use that window to ask for my mother, send messages, pass food, and on occasion send nudges and warnings when we were running late. We lost her to a devastating and unexpected traumatic brain bleed during the Fall of 2011. I can close my eyes and still hear her voice, see her hands, her smile, and above all, feel her love. My abuela remains in my heart; I miss her dearly and wish my own children had the benefit of more time with her.

The adjustment to my new environment wasn't hard. I learned to love Maracay as my own in no time. Maracay is known for its parks, its zoo, Las Delicias avenue, the bay of CATA and the beaches of Choroní and Cuyagua, La Maestranza Cesar Giron (a small but colorful bullfighting arena in the middle of the city) and last but not least, the many military bases scattered throughout the whole state. I became me in Maracay; I left my childhood behind to become a young adult, a passionate defender of social justice, a terrible but truthful writer, a dork about things of the heart, and a devoted Catholic.

As time passed, spending the weekends at the homes of my aunts and uncles became part of my regular routine. These trips allows me to grow close to my cousins, especially Anhwar, Khrysmari, Khrystabel and Ana Mariela. Since Anhwar and I were born only a day apart, we would celebrate birthdays together; we also went to the same elementary and high school, shared long weekends at my grandma's, and would stay at each others home for days during Christmas, summer break or any other long weekend we could. We are a very close family and even now, despite the fact that half of us live in exile, we remain very close.

I started sixth grade at San Juan Bautista, which began the day as a very humble elementary school, then transformed into Pablo VI high school in the afternoon. The classrooms had half walls that allowed us to look out over the school's garden. In the middle of that garden stood a Venezuelan flag and the bust of our founding father, Simon Bolivar. The building had a metal roof without insulation which would force teachers to stop lectures every time it rained. There was no air conditioning and the only technology was a green blackboard where teachers and professors would give lectures, writing out the important bits of information in perfect cursive with the help of a simple piece of chalk.

I remained at Pablo VI until tenth grade, then spent eleventh and final year in a different school, Dr. Gustavo H. Machado High School. It was closer to our house and held its classes during the morning. Though it was a bit smaller than Pablo VI, there was more exposure to music and art. In the Venezuelan education system, there is no such thing as Middle School. Elementary school begins with kindergarten and ends with sixth grade. High school starts with seventh grade and continues through eleventh; there is no twelfth grade, a fact that would prove relevant for me later in life.

If I had to share my immediate recollections of each school that I was part of, I would say that La Asuncion was a small playground, Rómulo Gallegos was a bigger playground, San Juan Bautista gave me my first kiss, Pablo VI my first love and G.H. Machado my first poem.

Life in Venezuela wasn't always easy, though. My Godfather Ruben is one of the most important spiritual mentors in my life. My Padrino was a monk from Los Hermanos De La Cruz Blanca, a congregation of San Francisco de Asis. Their work is very similar to that of the Mother Theresa of Calcutta. They served everyone in need, housed the homeless, cared for the ill and the handicapped, donated to the poor, fed the hungry, and provided clothing, refuge or simply a place to pray to any person that knocked on their door. I had the privilege to be a volunteer in their house and to go in a mission trip that changed my life and marked my soul.

We traveled to a town called Cocorote in the state of Yaracuy. During that trip, when I was only fifteen years of age, I witnessed misery on a level many could never comprehend. Being poor took on a whole new meaning in my life; all of the sudden the phrases "having nothing" and "being hungry" came with the memory of haunted faces. The meaning of the word service changed my life forever. I realized that just being able to walk was an unreachable dream for many, and with that, I discovered the joy of being healthy. I took a good look at myself and started counting my blessings. During that trip, my faith gave me smiles in the middle of tragedy, happiness between walls of sadness, light in moments of darkness, and peace it the middle of storms. Definitely, my time in Maracay and my trip to Cocorote taught me life lessons that have shaped me in ways too numerous to count.

After High School, I went back to Valencia and moved in with my father (Jesus Sr), my step-mom (Piri), and my two brothers (Gustavo and Guillermo). My plan was to study medicine and follow the footsteps of my grandfather's Miguel, whom I called Papapa. As you may already know by now, we may have plans for our lives, but life usually has other ideas in mind—often ideas that are very different than ours. But if we pay close attention, these sidetracks always seem to make perfect sense at the end of the road; we just don't see it while we are building it. My attempt at a medical career is the perfect example of this phenomenon.

In 1998, right after high school ended, I was inspired and excited. I was so eager to go to college. I had my paperwork ready, school transcripts and reference letters in hand, and even a cover letter and resume that were more like a small autobiography. I felt as if my dream of becoming a doctor were just beyond the horizon and I was ready to reach for it. Yet in all my excitement, there was a problem. Somehow, as crazy as it may sound, I missed the deadline to register and take the admission exam for medical school. By the time I realized what I'd done—or not done for that matter—it was too late and there was nothing I could do to correct the mistake.

That was a huge disappointment, not only for myself, but for my entire family. On my father's side of the family, Papapa is a doctor, my grandmother Blanca (Ita) is a nurse, my uncle Carlos is a surgeon and my aunt Esmeralda a psychiatrist. Needless to say the pressure and expectations were high. On my mother's side of the family, I was to be the first doctor of the family. I'll never erase the memory of my mother's face when I had to tell her I was not going to start school that year. I could see the emotions playing out as if they were a sad poem being retold as I explained that I could not attend, not because I hadn't made the cut, but because I just missed the deadline to turn in paperwork.

I just could not believe it happened to me. I was so sure of my plans, I could already see myself being a doctor, having patients, helping people, and making a difference in people's lives. It felt unnatural to me, as if I were suddenly in the script of some strangers life, as if the universe should have known that missing my deadline was not suppose to happen. I was heartbroken.

It took me awhile to get over the feeling of defeat and disbelief. But surely enough, the confident nature of a teenager wasn't going to let that slow me down. I was still eager to start something, do something. I wanted to become somebody, I just didn't know how. Looking back, I am amazed at how significant that chain of events has been on my life.

Since admission exams for medical school were given only once a year, I had to find something to make my days productive and feel like I was moving forward and not getting stuck. I knew that If I didn't make it to school that year, my chances of making it the following one would drop dramatically. For me, it was all about timing. I imagine it is similar to a minor league athlete who feels his chances of making it to the pro's slip further away with every day that he is not already there, in the game. I also felt like if I spent one day without studying, learning and preparing myself to be a doctor, I was going to lose out completely by failing the test when the chance finally did arrive. It was time to do something.

My grandparents, Papapa and Ita had a Non-Governmental Organization (NGO) called ASOVOSS (Asociacion de Voluntarios de Salud Social) which, when translated, means Volunteer Association of Social Health. This NGO offered classes to prepare people to be the equivalent of a Certified Nurse Assistant (CNA), Emergency Medical Technician (EMT), social workers or community organizers. At that time, my grandparents were getting ready to start a new set of classes and without a doubt, I asked them if I could be one of their students. Papapa would be in charge of the social classes and Ita would be in charge of the medical education. I quickly registered for both. I enjoyed both classes. I found the way to calm my thirst for helping others by becoming an EMT/CNA with the help of my grandmother, and a social worker/community organizer under the careful mentoring of my grandfather.

My mother suggested I finish an English course which I'd started but never finished a few years before. It was a very intense course with an emphasis on grammar offered by the University of Carabobo. I realized I wanted to complete the course, and that I also wanted to become more proficient in computers, so I enrolled in a computer course as well. My weekly schedule was pretty busy. Mondays and Wednesdays were my computer classes in the mornings and my grandfather's lectures in the afternoon. Tuesdays and Thursdays were my English classes in the mornings and my grandmother's lectures in the afternoon. I took Fridays to travel back to Maracay to visit my mother and my highschool sweetheart.

During that year, I learned that compassion was the core of health care thanks to the soft and tender care of my grandmother Ita. I learned to negotiate my way through arguments and debates. I got to know my grandparents in a way that will leave a permanent mark in my heart. Papapa taught me that strength is not measured by pure force but by the absence of it; that a gentle giant is way more persuasive than a little bully. I learned the importance of education as a tool to rise out of poverty, embraced knowledge as a form of enrichment, and recognized that respect was the basic need for evening the playing field between the weak and the strong.

I also met Mr. Villegas, a close friend of my grandfather and a man that transmitted his love and passion for history and politics with every conversation. He would turn an afternoon cup of coffee into an amazing Venezuelan history lesson, told with a passion that only a true historian would have. He would sound as if he was there at the time of Bolivar, or in the middle of crucial moments in modern Venezuelan history. A quick drive to downtown would become a lecture on national or global politics. His understanding of current events was given to me through the filter of his conservative, right-leaning vision while my grandfather's was shared through his more moderate and liberal beliefs.

They made a good team. Papapa was a bit tall, with white skin and a white mustache. He wore brown glasses; his hands were always clean and his nails perfectly trimmed. His standard wardrobe included a beige jacket and a brown hat, a white guayabera, beige dress pants, a brown belt and brown dress shoes—all topped off with a brown leather messenger bag that contained all his important papers. He was soft spoken, slow in his pace, concrete and certain of every single step he made. Noble and kind, yet firm and disciplined.

Mr. Villegas was a bit shorter, with white hair that circled his head but bald on top. He wore round black glasses, long sleeve shirts and a black leather jacket. He always carried his .38 revolver on his waist as his lone accessory. His voice was deep; his speech was eloquent and entertaining. He commanded respect with his presence. He had strong views and solid convictions. Mr. Villegas was the iron spear, and my grandfather was the steady and savvy hand that knew when and how to handle it.

Together, they managed to impress upon me a sense of respect and admiration for their wisdom and dedication to their cause, their work ethics, responsibility and impeccable way of being. They wouldn't always agree, but usually managed to come to a sort of mutual truce until one overcame the other. Sometimes it was my grandfather's power of persuasion, others, it was Mr. Villegas strong will. In the end, the biggest lesson I learned was perseverance, a trait they both had plenty of. Together, they made me hungry for knowledge and thirsty for helping others and left me eager to venture into life.

By mid 1999 I was almost done with the courses I'd taken to pass the time. I'd grown closer to my father, my step mom and my brothers, especially to my mentors; Papapa, Ita, and Mr. Villegas, yet I was finally getting ready to take my admission test for medical school. This time, the deadline to turn in my paperwork did not pass me by and I felt confident I was going to make it.

That was when life changed my plans once again. I was devastated when I found out I didn't get the grade I needed in order to be accepted into medical school. It was very tough to face the fact that I apparently did not have what it took academically to pursue my dream career. I didn't know what to do. All I wanted was to be a doctor; my passion was medicine. Worse, I'd excelled in almost everything I had undertaken so far in life and for the first time I realized that the real world is far more competitive than I'd expected—and that sometimes life is simply unfair.

With the resolve only found in the young, I bounced back. I decided I wasn't going to let that test stop me from getting into medical school—I put on my fighting gloves and set out to get what I thought should have been mine. I made phone calls, gathered letters of recommendation, revamped my resume and added my latest courses, wrote a heartbreaking cover letter and then I visited school officials, professors, janitors...everybody. They got to know me very well in the Medical Department of the University. Despite my efforts, at the end of those days and weeks, I still went back home without a letter of acceptance.

Still unwilling to let go of my dream, I discovered that there was another way in, a last resort. The University would allow a certain number of students with extraordinary talents in sports, arts, or special skills to be enrolled in their programs. I played indoor soccer all through high school; I would only have to go to the tryouts and give my best.

I considered myself a pretty good player though I was only able to play for some minor league clubs. However, I knew that it was my only chance at gaining admission. No matter my skill level, I had another problem: I hadn't played soccer for at least a year. I'd started swimming with a small team at a local club shortly after moving in with my father, and with everything else going on in my life, soccer became just a few games between friends after swimming practices. How could I have known that soccer might have been my ticket to medical school? I knew I wasn't prepared but once again I buckled down and pushed forward.

The day to showcase my abilities as a soccer player came and I headed to the tryouts. It was a clear morning, hot and sunny, and the assessments were taking place on an open basketball court with concrete floors, nothing really new to me. The university coach was there, along with other coaches and that day, the state team was practicing with the university team. Needless to say, I was truly intimidated by the caliber of players there. Some of them were wearing the national colors, clearly indicating that they had played at national level. The coach seemed uninterested—perhaps even annoyed—by my presence. In the middle of the match, in what felt like an act of pity, I was given the chance to enter the game.

I just wanted to show them my best. I wanted a chance to score, make a good pass or assist, slide on the concrete, scraping my knee but blocking the tallest and fastest forward rival player. I only wanted one move, one second, one chance. It never came.

I was seventeen years old, about five feet seven inches, maybe a hundred and thirty pounds. I was no match for any of the state team players. I actually think the cheerleaders could have taken me out with a single kick if they'd wanted. I barely remember touching the ball but I do remember falling about five times. It was awful and embarrassing. I was not allowed to play much and the coach quickly got me out of the match. As I approached him to ask for another chance, maybe drills or shooting the ball, he quickly disregarded me and said: "Just go home. What are you still doing here?"

It made me stop in my tracks. What was I doing there? At the time, I couldn't think of an answer to that question. I'd run in circles for so long that I had forgotten why I was running in the first place. I didn't answer the coach. I remained silent, all the noise of the court going quite as I just stood there with a blank stare on my face. After a few moments, I gathered myself together and left.

On the way back home I thought about my idea of life. I began doubting myself and what I'd believed I was up to that point. For the first time I began to realize that I might not get to be what I wanted to be. Maybe I wasn't as smart as I thought, maybe I didn't have what was needed to be a doctor, maybe both. Was it a result of not being honest with myself? Did I think I could accomplish more than I was actually capable of? I didn't know the answer, but I knew I wasn't going to be starting medical school that year—or any other.

It was yet another blow for my family, another disappointment in my life. Yet without realizing what path I'd embarked on, I'd learned skills and obtained tools that would become essential for my future. At the time, it seemed as if I merely wanted to stay busy and productive as I recovered from life's repeated blows. Looking back, though, I can see how my life makes perfect sense, with my victories and defeats mingling along with my plans and dreams to shape my current reality.

With my dreams of medical school dead, I had to find a new goal, a new plan. I'd taken the news hard and pretty much given up on pursuing a medical career. I was mentally exhausted. I visited my mother in Maracay and while I was there, she and my Dad offered to pay for me to go to law school. It was a private and expensive university; I didn't think my parents would be able to afford it, but they said they would try.

I went back to Valencia to speak to my father and tell him about my plans to go back to Maracay to study law. He seemed surprised and not too happy about it. I'd somewhat expected his reaction, but was unprepared for my grandfather's. I remembered going to his house and telling him about my new intentions of studying law. I actually asked him for help as I knew my parents were going to have a real hard time paying for tuition. He was visibly upset. He was angry at the university, at his friends at the faculty but above all, he was mad at me for making the decision to study law. I felt as if I was telling him I was going to study to become a thief. He was mad and disappointed, even more than when I failed the admission test for medical school. He simply told me "law is not for you". He actually tried to convince me to stay in Valencia and try once again the following year to get into medical school. It seemed too much and too far for me. A whole year? In "teenager time" that was a lifetime.

That's when he announced, "I am not paying for something I know you will not like. Law is not a career for you".

I don't remember the details of the rest of the conversation, all I remember is that he was angry with my decision and very clear that law was going to make me unhappy.

A bit shaken but still resolved, I left Valencia only to find a whole new set of challenges in Maracay at my mother's house. My dad's business was not doing very well and they were barely able to make the first tuition payment. The stress was visible and I didn't like to be a burden on my parents. I still had three sisters in school that truly needed their help. With eighteen years on me, I felt I needed to start adding to the household income. To make matters worse, my dad had become the president of the homeowner association in the apartment building that we lived in and that brought unwanted political attention to our family, proving to be dangerous and a decisive moment to our family at the end.

Law school seems to have been no more than a brief moment in time. I was more worried about the stress I was putting onto my parents than how well I was doing in my classes. I did enjoy law school though, or at least the idea of me becoming a lawyer. However, things at home where changing rapidly. Our lives became more a matter of survival than anything else. Now that I was becoming an adult, I was more aware of real issues in our family. All of the sudden I could see my parents struggle to make ends means. I could see how tired my dad really was, my mother's stress, and the sacrifices they made every single day to make sure that we had food and a chance to a decent education. They understood what education meant. They were, and still are, the living proof of how much tougher life could be without education.

The position my dad held as the president of the homeowner association was supposed to be more an administration job than anything else. But with the social climate of Venezuela at that time, that position became a political battleground and a power struggle for junior political players. An argument about budget and expenses would turn into political discussions and accusations of partisan strategies that were never there. Paranoia and false accusations could end up with somebody going to jail for no reason at all. Even something as simple as a regularly scheduled meeting could be seen as an illegal assembly intending to overthrow the current government. Chavez supporters quickly and erroneously started feeling that any position, as small as it could appear, could be used to secure Chavez Revolution.

It was known among our circle of friends that my family was clearly not supportive of the Chavez Revolution, and in a bizarre turn of events, Chavez supporters began to systematically sabotage people's means of earning a living. In the blink of an eye, threatening, harassment and extortion became the norm in a new post-democracy Venezuela—and we were their target.

Threatening phone calls came at all hours, insulting notes were left on our cars and even began appearing on our front doors. People began to insult and argue with us inside the elevators, lobby and even in the parking lot. It was the beginning of what became the most crucial moments in our lives, moments that made my parents realize that they might have to leave everything they'd worked for and flee to protect our family.

My dad received the worst of a regime that rewarded violence, though we were all victims of violent acts. Fear was with us day in and day out. Everyone was feeling the wrath of a system that protected those supporting the Revolution but disregarded the rest of Venezuelans, a system that initially called itself a Revolution and is now falsely referred to as Socialism.

There was a pivotal event that changed my parents lives forever, a day that none of us will ever forget: my dad was assaulted, kidnapped, mugged and left for dead in a dark ally in one of the worst neighborhoods of Valencia. He was clearly warned about not reporting the event and told to leave.

To leave. They didn't mean the building we were living in, nor the city or the state, but the country itself. He was told to simply disappear or they would finish what they'd begun.

After that day, we were in stealth mode. We were even scared to make noise in our home. We would leave home early in the morning for school and would not come back until late at night, praying nobody would see us. Being home was no longer pleasant. It didn't feel safe. It didn't feel like home anymore. I remember a day when my mother came to me and asked me: if there was a time that we had to leave, would you leave with us?

The question seemed ridiculous. "Of course!" I said. They were my parents and I would do whatever I was told. I didn't see what my parents were seeing, didn't understand that they knew I might not want to leave my school or my highschool sweetheart behind. Instead, I saw my parents struggles, the everyday fights, threats, harassment and bullying they faced. It was a nightmare for me as well. I honestly didn't think twice about it.

America! Really?

That was my reaction. A smile on my face, a deep breath, and a long hug to my mother.

The following weeks, our house became emptier and emptier with every day that passed. My parents sold some of our stuff but most of it was just given away to our family. Furniture, appliances, clothing, our computer, the stereo, pictures, letters, birthday cards, bicycles, school uniforms, food, kitchen utensils, my sister's toys, they all disappeared. Anything and everything that did not fit in a suitcase vanished.

We contacted a family member in the Venezuelan Army who knew about military logistic flights that flew out of Maracay to Miami. They carried supplies for Venezuelan military personnel who were training in America. According to our relative, the flights would depart every Wednesday. We weren't able to get a specific flight date, though, and wouldn't know when we were leaving until the day before of the actual flight. That meant we had to had our bags ready, day after day, week after week as we waited for the call.

We reached a point of no return. We'd given everything away, sold some of it, rented our apartment, sold our car, and were living out of suitcases. My sisters were excited about "the trip". They weren't aware of our intentions of leaving Venezuela for good.

I spent my last days in Venezuela saying my goodbyes, giving hugs, trying to capture every moment, every smile, every kiss. I can remember the last night, the heartbreaking goodbyes of my closest friends and family followed by a few measly hours of restless sleep. I knew that the next day was the beginning of a new journey and a whole new life for all of us.

CHAPTER TWO

*"EMIGRATION, FORCED OR CHOSEN, ACROSS NATIONAL
FRONTIERS OR FROM VILLAGE TO METROPOLIS,
IS THE QUINTESSENTIAL EXPERIENCE OF OUR TIME."*
— BRITISH ART CRITIC AND POET, JOHN BERGER.

I can still remember that day in crystalline detail; I can close my eyes and feel the rush of emotions from that long-ago morning. It's one of those life experiences so charged with adrenaline and intensity that writes an indelible print upon not just your memory, but your soul. It was a day that will stay with me for the rest of my life.

The morning started early. I remember my parents' faces lined with fear, the blank stare on my own face, and the excitement of my three sisters. At 6:00 a.m. we said the last goodbyes to our family outside the airport. I had the typical and movie-like run and kiss from my girlfriend by the side of the road. As we drove away, I left behind the promises of a teenager in love, the innocence in our eyes, the most pure and naive belief that love can conquer all, and the hope of a dreamer.

It was still very dark and a little cold. We made some last minute phone calls and cried some more. I remember approaching the gate at the base and looking back to see some of my family members and my girlfriend at the end of the road. It all seemed so surreal. Military Police guards checked our names on a list and pointed out the building where we were supposed to go. The gate opened and we entered Venezuelan Military Air Base "Base Aerea Libertador".

It was nothing like the international airport that I'd imagined the night before. It was a typical military base—clean, neat, utilitarian, simple, and surrounded by one story buildings. We entered the building we'd been directed to and sat down in a waiting room. Shortly after we arrived, more military personnel checked our paperwork and our luggage, then we were told to exit the building through the back door and wait outside. I was surprised to find out that behind that door were the hangars.

Sunrise found us standing outside along the back of the building. I could see a handful of F16s, helicopters and other planes I couldn't identify. There was a helicopter getting ready to take off at the end of the hangars and I could also see a "Hercules" warming up its engines. Once again we were directed to present our luggage and a military police K9 soldier brought his German shepherd over to examine them. Meanwhile I could hear the engines from the Hercules get louder and louder. We asked a military policeman where our plane was and he pointed right at that incoming cargo plane.

At around eight that morning, as I sat inside a very noisy and cold Hercules C130 from Venezuelan Air Force at "Libertador" Air Base, flying somewhere over Venezuela, I suddenly realized I'd just left everything behind. I sat down against the wall of the plane, between two aluminum poles with green webbing and a small window behind my head. There were no chairs or restrooms, just a pile of supplies attached to the floor of the plane and a little lap belt to strap ourselves down, with no armrest or headrest. I could see all the wiring of the plane and some blinking lights. As you can imagine, this was no ordinary flight.

We were not the only family traveling either. I was trying not to make eye contact with anybody, as my eyes were swollen from only two hours of sleep and all the crying from the night before. I was just trying to look tough inside that big, cold plane. The temperature continued to drop; it got so cold that one of the crew members took his jacket off and offered it to my two youngest sisters. The plane was so noisy that I couldn't talk with anybody, even if I'd wanted to. It didn't really matter; I didn't have anything to say anyway. I kept turning around, staring out the window, dreaming about my future and already reminiscing about my past.

After approximately four hours of miserable flight time, we finally landed at Miami International Airport. The little door on the side of the airplane opened and we got out of the plane right in the middle of a runway. We were directed to walk down the runway toward the main building and go up some stairs, then mix in with the regular incoming passengers from other flights. We starting walking through the airport and I started feeling like my life was happening in slow motion.

We arrived at the line leading to the immigration checkpoint. It was a tense moment for my parents and I. My sisters couldn't stop smiling, but my mom could barely stop crying and my dad was physically shaking. Everything was still in slow motion. I couldn't hear anything but the sound of my own breathing. I couldn't see anything past 10 feet in front of me. I was numb; I couldn't feel my feet. I was shocked by a mix of emotions and overwhelming sensations. I remember looking forward to getting a good night of sleep at a place I could call home. Little did I know I was still three weeks away from those simple dreams.

I honestly don't remember how long we waited in line to go through the immigration checkpoint. Standing there I couldn't help but wonder— what if? What if we have to go back? What if we don't make it? What if I hate it? What if I love it, but my family hates it? What if my parents were right and moving to a totally different country and leaving everything behind was the best decision of our lives? What if they were wrong?

Finally, it was my dad's turn. I walked with him in case he needed help translating only to find out that American immigration officers are fluent in Spanish.

"Are you here for business or pleasure?"

"How long are you planning to stay?"

"How many are traveling with you?"

Those were some of the routine questions my dad was asked. He handed over the passports and after a short inspection, they were sealed and handed back to my dad.

"Bienvenidos a Estados Unidos".

I let out a breath I hadn't even realized I was holding as we moved past the checkpoint. On our way to pick up our suitcases, I started noticing one of the most beautiful aspects of this country, the "Melting Pot". It was the typical rush of noon-time at an International Airport. People were coming and going, some saying hello, others saying good bye. There were tall people, short people, white, black and some in between. There were no more signs in Spanish, and even the loudspeakers reminded me that I was no longer home.

Once outside, I found myself just staring at people, and definitely more relaxed now. I was able to pay attention to details like the incredibly hot air that slapped my face as soon as the exit doors of the airport opened, the amount of traffic, and the smell of asphalt and oil from the ground. We picked up a rental minivan and my dad decided to take us through South Beach. I sat in silence, trying to take in everything I was seeing.

The highway looked whiter, wider and the cars seemed faster. Since the only car we had in Venezuela was a navy blue Fiat Uno, spotting the big SUVs, semi trucks, and the occasional limousines was exciting. I noticed the beautiful Miami Beach and its glass high-rises, the palm trees, sea grapes, and pine trees on each side of the road. We pulled over and realized that the sand wasn't that nice—I couldn't walk barefoot on it and it smelled strange. By that time we were starving, so we set out to find food. Can you guess what our first meal in America was? I hope you guessed Burger King.

Trying to use a phone card to call our family and let them know we'd arrived safely was our first adventure. I didn't know what the pin number was or when to enter it; I couldn't understand the recorded voice or dial the numbers at the right time. Putting gasoline in the minivan was another funny story. We pulled up to the pump and just waited and waited for the guy to come and fill up our tank. After sitting there for a while we realized that people seemed to fill up their tanks by themselves. And that became our next adventure...paying for gas. Looking back now, I can see the humor in the situation, but at that point in time, well, let's just say that there was a lot of yelling through the speaker at the pump between us and the poor guy working at the gas station. We learned how expensive gasoline was compared to what we were used to paying and ended up making several trips to the inside of the store before everything was sorted out.

We didn't really stop at South Beach, we just drove through. My dad didn't know how long it was going to take us to travel from there to his cousin's house in Palm Beach, so he got on I-95 North and headed that way. While my dad drove, we were trying to spot the best looking cars in the highway. My sisters' faces could tell a few stories, they were full of excitement, looking out the windows and asking rapid-fire questions about Disney. That was the moment my parents decided to ask my sisters if one day, they would like to live in a country like this one. After only few seconds, they all exclaimed "Yes!" With such a rousing response, my parents finally broke the news...though they still held back a bit "Well, we would like to stay here too. We may not go back to Venezuela".

I watched my sisters begin to go through the same emotions that I'd been experiencing for the past several months. To this date, I don't know if they felt lied to or tricked by my parents. I remembered just back a couple of days before, my sisters were asking my mother to make sure all their toys would go untouched while they were away at Disney. They never had the chance to say goodbye to their friends or even our family the same way I did. I hoped they were too young to care or notice. If not, I hoped time would heal any scars or resentment toward my parents or life itself.

There were several people that helped us tremendously, especially during the beginning. One of them was my dad's cousin, Cesar. He offered us the use of his house while we got accustomed to our new lives. Cesar and his wife Adriana gave us not only advice and orientation but the support and confidence that everybody needed, guiding us on everything from traffic laws to how much money we should carry with us.

There was so much to do, so much to get used to, so many questions. It's not that Venezuela is so very different when it comes to daily life, but there are certainly language and cultural differences. Just to give an example, about two weeks into my new life, I walked in a gas station and got a hotdog. The clerk asked me if I wanted a soda with it and I answered back "no, thanks, I'll just have a Pepsi". In my mind, soda was the sparkly bottled water that tasted like alka-seltzer, something no kid wanted any part of when growing up.

Several days after that, a coworker asked me if I wanted a soda, I shook my head and asked him why people here liked so much soda, and he said "They're cheap". Finally, some time after that, my dad's cousin asked me if I wanted a soda and I had to ask…. "What the hell is up with people here in America, don't you guys like Coke or Pepsi, Sprite or 7up?" He lost it laughing, and then told me "here, soda means soft drinks or fountain drinks like Coke or Pepsi, not just soda water."
I finally understood why I'd gotten so many weird looks when I said "no" to sodas but welcomed an iced cold Coca-cola.

After about a week in Cesar's house, we moved to Stuart, a smaller and less crowded town about 40 miles north of Palm Beach. There, another of my dad's cousin, Rihber, offered us yet another helping hand. My mother was also introduced to Mrs. Nancy, an angel that took pride in helping others, especially immigrants and those with nothing or very little in life. I remember her telling my mother about churches and other places that served free food and provided cheap clothes and furniture. So, every weekday my mom would take us to different churches for dinner and we also became very familiar with stores like Goodwill and the Salvation Army.

By the end of October, only a month after our arrival, we'd accomplished a lot, but my own reality wasn't quite what I'd dreamed it would be. In some ways, it was better and faster than anticipated, in others ways, I found that there were obstacles that slowed me down. Isn't life just like that; you have a plan and imagine things are going to happen in a certain way, then later you realize that life has a mind of its own and you are just a player learning the rules of the game. Only now it looked like it was time to play a whole new game.

Everything was happening so fast. Every day brought new challenges: finding a job, getting a place to live, registering for school, finding an attorney, getting driver licenses, buying a car, buying groceries, connecting the power, calling the city to set up the water account, getting a phone line, finding school supplies, buying bicycles (our only form of transportation while we saved for a car). We would start planning our days by finding out if we could use somebody's car. If no car was available, we had to use the bicycles to run local errands.

I had particular goals that I wanted to reach. As I mentioned before, I had a plan, to say the least, a very simple and naïve plan. My idea of how I'd reach my dreams was almost comical when I think back on it: Go to the American Embassy, get a Visa, go to America, register for high school, do well in sports, get a scholarship, go to college, become a doctor, lawyer or politician, find a job, get married, have children, and finally…. enjoy life. Pretty simple, right? America had so many options (or at least that's what I thought at the time) that it was actually hard for me to choose a career. I was certain of my future once again; it was all planned out, everything figured out. I didn't know exactly how I would get there, but I knew where I wanted to go.

The plan ran like a checklist through my brain. I'd accomplished the first three goals of my new life when I first landed in America—check, check and check—now on to the next: register for high school. I hadn't planned very well though, and registering at a high school was more challenging than I'd expected. I began to have doubts as I sat in front of a school counselor that didn't look too excited about me becoming his newest student. Then he gave me a list of reasons why he didn't think it was in my best interest to attend his school. First of all, I'd already turned 18 years old, pushing the age limit to be in school. I immediately countered with the fact that I had a neighbor that was older than me and attending that same high school. He quickly gave me his second reason: language skills. Although the interview was done entirely in English, he told me that my English wasn't good enough. I also refuted that statement, once again mentioning the neighbor as I pointed out how much better my English was compared to his.

At that point, I just wanted him to stop objecting and let me tell him what I had to offer. I was so ready to start giving my best, eager to adapt as quickly as possible. I wanted an opportunity to shine. I was good soccer player, a decent swimmer and I was willing to try my luck in baseball. I'd taken most of the classes needed to graduate—in fact, I was not only able to finish high school back in Venezuela but I was a first year law student in a private university.

It was the nail in the coffin. What I thought was going to be my best selling point turned out to be the final reason to dismiss my argument. In simple terms, I was not eligible to attend any high school because I had already received a high school diploma from another school.

I considered that my first failure, my first change in plans. I felt misunderstood and underappreciated. I was almost begging, pleading with the counselor. After seeing how upset I looked at the news, the counselor explained that there were other routes I could take in order to be able to attend college. I could do two things: I could take the TOEFL test (Test of English as a Foreign Language) or I could get my GED (commonly known as General Equivalency or General Education Diploma), then I would be eligible to go through the registration process of any college I wanted. He also referred me to an adult education center called "One Stop Career Center" where they could answer the questions I might have about the two different ways to get into college.

Honestly, I wasn't too excited about the idea of making either choice. For the TOEFL Test, I knew my English had to be pretty much perfect. To my mind, the test was a very difficult one, meant for geniuses who wanted to enter elite schools like Harvard, Princeton or Yale. I'd even heard of English speaking people not being able to pass it.

The other option sounded like the complete opposite. The GED Test was for people unable to complete high school. What I'd heard about Adult Learning Centers up to that point in my life was not good. I thought Learning Centers were for people who had learning disabilities, attention deficit disorders, had abused drugs or alcohol, or had other cognitive issues that forced them to drop school.

Neither of those routes were even slightly appealing at the time, but it turned out very different than expected. The TOEFL test is not as horrible as I thought, and of course there are students with learning disabilities and A.D.D, or drug and alcohol problems at the Learning Centers, but those are not the only reasons for someone to drop school. Life and society are far more complex and complicated than that. I learned that not everything is right or wrong, straight or not, black or white. Perhaps that helped me realize that I was here, in America. I made it and whatever happened, it would all be all right. It didn't matter all the loops and hoops I had to go through because I had options, I had a chance. And I was ready to take it.

CHAPTER THREE

"I challenge the Republican nominees and all Republicans to not just be the anti-illegal immigration party. That's not who we are and that's not who we should be, we should be the pro-legal immigration party."
— UNITED STATES SENATOR, MARCO RUBIO.

3.1

I could say that my challenges began with an internal battle between what I thought I was and what I actually had become here in America. Back in Venezuela I was a citizen, color blind, oblivious to others immigration issues. Here in America I didn't know the differences between a permanent resident and a citizen, I didn't even know my own race. I thought once you were a citizen, regardless of what country you came from or went to, you were always a citizen—I even thought I could check "white" on job applications. I was very young and very naïve. I believed American society was perfect. I didn't see darkness; I could not see evil.

I really miss those days, when I didn't know any racial slurs; when I could not distinguish the different accents within my own society, when I did not know the difference between a native and a foreigner and when I did not know about racism or prejudice. The more I learned the more complicated it got and the more confused I became. It was a time in my life when I was trying to adapt while learning the dynamics of a complex society. I was discovering what it meant to be an immigrant, its stigma and its challenges. In simple words, I was getting to know my new place in my new society.

Imagine this: you are at somebody's party and someone that lives in the house asks you to move your car out of the driveway. What would you do? Do you question his authority? Would you feel entitled to park on his driveway? Or would you just politely move your car? Now, imagine this, you actually live in the house and someone asks you to move your car from your own driveway. Would you feel the same way about the situation or do you question this person's authority? Would you just move your car from your own driveway with the same politeness? Or would you feel entitled to ask why and "Who is this guy?" That is the difference between a native and a foreigner. A native has a feeling of entitlement to the land he or she grew up in, and contrary to many peoples' beliefs, the foreigner does not have that same sense of entitlement, that feeling of freedom that we as Americans cherish so much.

I can write this because that is how I felt as an immigrant, I felt like I was at somebody's party, parked in someone else's driveway, not wanting to start any trouble and always willing to cooperate and help with anything.

Being in someone else's country is kind of like that; you try to be polite, not insult anybody, fly under the radar. You want to be incognito, to give something in return and hope for a chance to prove yourself in society. Yet all of this has to be balanced with your own needs, the things of importance to you and your way of life.

To me, education was the most significant tool for increasing my chances to succeed in life. Education is the foundation of my future and during my first months in America, getting that education was my number one priority. Although I encountered my first obstacle when I was not able to go to high school, I was still very focused and enthusiastic about my education and my chances to go to college. I wrestled with the different alternatives I had, and finally decided to give the "One Stop Career Center" the first chance. If the process turned out to be long and tedious, I would take my chances with the TOEFL instead.

Going to OSCC was the best choice I could have made at that time. I met a wonderful person and professor named Dee Ann DuBois. She was without a doubt what any student would want in a teacher. She was talented, patient, soft spoken, caring, and humble, simply an angel. She became my mentor and on many occasions my confidant. I remember the day I met her, telling her pretty much everything about me, maybe more than what she felt comfortable with at the time. She had to stop me from showing her things like my passport or explain to her my immigration status. It's just one of those things that I felt obligated to do in my situation. I wanted to be understood. I think at that time, if anybody would have stopped me on the street and asked me for an ID, I would have just taken it out of my wallet and naively handed to them.

Shortly after introducing myself to Miss Dee Ann, I started taking the initial tests to evaluate my level of education and how I would score on a possible GED test. Once she figured out my weaknesses and strengths, she crafted a study plan specifically for me. From that point on, I quickly started picking Miss Dee Ann's brain, brushing up on my English and the basics on math, social studies, science and American history. I was not required to go to class every day; in fact, Miss Dee Ann told me I could go and study whenever I wanted. Despite this, my desire to continue my education was all the motivation I needed to keep me going every afternoon. Every weekday after work I would ride about 5 miles on my bicycle to see Miss "D". I remember her ordering pizzas at night for all the students, most of the time with her own money. I would stay until closing time and then ride my bicycle another couple of miles home. I felt productive now that I was moving forward with a purpose and was pleased that, once again, I had a plan.

One night while taking one of the practice tests I noticed that the GED exam could be taken in three different versions, English, Canadian, or Spanish. Miss Dee Ann didn't think it would do any good to take the test in Spanish. She felt my focus should have been on learning and improving my English. I was so focused on trying to get back into college that I didn't pay attention to her suggestions, and by November of that same year, only two months after arriving in the States, I was taking the official Spanish version of the GED test.

I was feeling like things could start working themselves out. I was so excited about my GED test that after taking my exam, I visited a local college to find out the requirements to register and take classes. This time the college counselor was the one giving me bad news. Just as Miss Dee Ann feared, the Spanish version of the GED was not going to be sufficient to satisfy my English requirements. I needed to go back and take the English version of the GED.

At that point, I had two jobs and I was finally able to buy my first car, a 92' Ford Escort. I worked six days a week from 12pm to 5pm at one job and three to five days a week from 6pm to 2am at a second job. That meant not being able to go to OSCC at night and prepare for my English version of the GED test. Miss Dee Ann then told me about another professor that could help me. His name was Irenaldo "Ray" Garcia, a Cuban American professor who, like Miss Dee Ann, took pride in teaching, but in his case, with mostly immigrants. His office was located at another OSCC about 30 minutes away from where I lived, in a rural community called Indiantown. Professor Garcia was inspiring, full of energy, engaging, understanding and sympathetic when he heard my life story. He also made a study plan and we both started to work on it right away.

For the next few months, my day would start at 6:30am and finish at 2:00 am the following day. I would go to Mr. Garcia's classroom in the morning, then at noon, off to one of my jobs, and then, around 6pm off to another eight hours of work. Finally, by the time I would make it home, I was mentally and physically exhausted. The only thing keeping me going forward was my deepest desire to go to college and the motivation I would get from witnessing my own family's struggles.

Indiantown was a humbling experience, my personal eye opener. Indiantown is a rural community where there is only the main road with its handful of shops and gas stations, one fire station, few law enforcement officers and a large immigrant population. It's populated by mostly low income families, schools in need of supplies and resources, dirt roads, a railroad that passes right beside the main road of the town, a lot of pickup trucks and domestic animals like dogs, cats and chickens running free on the streets. I saw a lot of poverty and the harsh living conditions that I thought I left behind.

At the Indiantown OSCC, the classroom was filled with people that had so little, mostly Guatemalans and Mexicans and every single one of them with a remarkable story. Their eyes looked tired, with dirt from work under their nails, their arms and faces scarred from working the fields and wearing clothes several sizes bigger or smaller.

I thought I was going through a bad time until I heard some of their stories. Most of them were undocumented, leaving husband, wives or children behind in their homelands. They lived and worked in deplorable conditions. Some would share a room with two or three other people, with no transportation other than a bicycle and their jobs were all on farms and in citrus groves. Housekeepers, nannies, farmers, construction workers, yard workers, roofers, anything that was hard labor. That's what I call black collar jobs, the ones that not many people even consider doing. There I was, living in a modest but clean apartment, two jobs, and a car. Almost all my immediate family accompanying me every step of the way and I still found myself occasionally crying and homesick.

I was able to compare both schools and their students. Back at the Stuart OSCC where Miss Dee Ann was, I met other kinds of people. It was a more urban setting and less crowded. There were not that many undocumented workers. Most of the students there were teenagers and young adults with difficult childhoods, school dropouts, troubled kids and homeless people, trying to get a fresh start, or simply a career change. There, I got to see and hear once again how it is to live in a bad neighborhood, where at least one of your parents is into drugs or alcohol, and where domestic violence is commonly an unpunished crime.

A clear example was a student I met. She was a 16 year old mother who dropped out of school when she was only 13. Her dad was incarcerated and her mother lost custody of her due to alcoholism. She was left with her grandfather who was verbally and physically abusive as well. With little to no supervision she spent most of her time on the streets of her neighborhood. Surrounded by drugs, alcohol and prostitution she soon lost interest in school and eventually got pregnant. The baby's father got thrown in jail for drug possession and some other charges. The boyfriend she had at the time was also a drug dealer and abusive to her and her baby as well. Her home was in terrible shape, a broken down trailer with old furniture, a permanent cigarette stench, dirty and with food, clothes and beer cans everywhere. Definitely not a place to raise a baby.

I realized something that most people would simply miss: a different set of needs in the harsh living conditions between the two towns and their implications for future generations. In Indiantown, there were migrant workers with "no real chances" in life, limited resources and ignored by most of us. They were a group of people and part of our society that crossed the border just to find another set of life lasting limitations. On the other side of town, Stuart had the others with a "slim chance" in life. Those who share the same freedom and liberties that most of us enjoy but their surroundings are like moving sands, keeping most of them from enjoying the results of hard and honest work and condemning them to a social and cultural battle where they are clearly at a disadvantage.

I ask you now what I asked myself back then: what real chances does 'Jose' from Indiantown have in life without education; without the support and motivation of his family because they are thousands of miles away? How tough would it be to find a decent job without a social security number or a 'green card'? How much tougher would life be without a driver license? What about riding a bicycle everywhere you go? How many groceries can you carry on a bike? How much would you miss your wife, or husband, or children while being away in a different country picking oranges for 12 hours a day? What slim chance does 'Jessica' from Stuart have in life without education? How motivated would somebody be with the constant verbal and physical abuse of his or her grandfather? How much harder it would be for a teenager to stay out of trouble when surrounded by drugs and alcohol? How hard it would be to raise your child in either community? Which set of needs and limitations would you prefer to have?

After seeing all that, I was not feeling so unfortunate anymore, I was more grateful for all the things I had. I started enjoying more my parents and sisters' company, and definitely enjoyed the benefit of having my own car. I thanked my parents for saving the money needed to pay for the immigration process that so many didn't even have access to. I also thanked my parents for putting me through good schools and giving me the education I needed to face the challenges in life.

Life has an extraordinary way of writing itself straight on bent lines, and just when I was getting comfortable with the idea of getting a GED in order to go to college, life gave me another set of challenges, something that changed all my circumstances in life and took almost everything away from me.

My biggest battle, my biggest struggle, was something unforeseen and unavoidable. We were all working towards obtaining our permanent resident status, but we didn't understand how tricky and fragile that status could be, and to be honest I didn't quite understand the whole process of obtaining the visas. The day of my arrival into the U.S, we were all given what is known as an "I-94", it was a little piece of paper, sealed by an immigration officer that showed the days we are allowed to stay legally in the U.S. Typically, somebody that shows up in the airport with a tourist visa like we did, gets up to six months to stay per visit, sometimes one week or two months, it all depends on the immigration officer's discretion.

The tourist visa that I got at the American embassy in Venezuela was set to expire by July 2005 but, the "I94" that the immigration officer gave us the day of our arrival was set to expire after six months. This meant that whatever my parents had to or wanted to do, it had to happen before that. To the best of my knowledge, my dad was trying to obtain a business visa. It required a well established Venezuelan company to open a franchise here in the U.S. With my dad as the manager of the franchise, the rest of the family could remain here past the I-94's deadline. By January 2001, some frictions with the owner of the company in Venezuela kept my dad from being able to open the franchise here. The process was slow, and with deadlines that needed to be met, in some cases from one day to another. It was also challenging because the company's owner became defensive when he had to provide personal information about his private life, business and finances.

By mid February, we were running out of options as we found ourselves without a Venezuelan company to sponsor my dad. Sometime in March, I was a "somebody", a teenager with nothing to fear, working, studying, still adapting... the next day, I became a "nobody". I did not have the right kind of citizenship, or even a permanent residency; I did not know how long I was going to be able to live in U.S, I was fearful, and once again, trying to adapt to the sudden changes of my circumstances.

Being a nobody is not an overstatement. Staying past my "I-94" deadline meant becoming an illegal. There would be no differences between me and somebody that crossed the Arizona desert or swam across Rio Grande in Texas. That sympathy I felt for my fellow English students in Indiantown became my very own reality. Their fears became my fears, their limitations became my limitations, their challenges became my challenges and their chances in life became the same chances I would have to succeed.

I was overwhelmed with mixed feelings. On one hand I felt humiliated, on the other I was frightened and uncertain about my future like never before. I felt abandoned by someone or something, without any protection, like being naked in the middle of Times Square. And, to a certain degree, I felt discriminated against.

Our attorney told my parents that if we were to lose our immigration status by staying past our March deadline, we would not be able to apply for any other immigration process. Moreover, if we decided to leave United States after losing our status, we would be banned from coming back for the next five to ten years. Those were the kind of decisions that we were facing. Going back to the Chavez regime was not an option, but staying meant becoming an undocumented immigrant and not being able to leave until we could fix our immigration status which could take years or even decades. For a lot of immigrants, staying undocumented in United States is actually better than going back to their homelands. That presents the likely risk of undergoing and tolerating abuses and harsh conditions that we wouldn't tolerate in different circumstances. For other immigrants, living in United States with all the limitations that being undocumented presents, is simply not worth it.

For example, in some cases an undocumented immigrant from Colombia,

Costa Rica or Chile would feel compelled to go back to his or her own country and not deal with the difficulties and limitations of living in America without immigration status, whereas undocumented immigrants from Guatemala, Mexico, or Haiti, if returned, would have a quality of life far worse than it is here in the States, even as undocumented immigrants. In our case, returning to Venezuela meant not only a worse quality of life, but our very own lives would be at risk thanks to the political intolerance of the Chavez's regime.

It was without a doubt another important and crucial decision in our lives. For my parents, it was a decision that could affect not only their future but my sisters and mine. My parents had to decide what was better for their children, to take a chance on life or death in communist Venezuela or to take our chances in America as undocumented? Do we bet our future on our homeland's limitations and imperfections or bet on the United States, the land of opportunities and freedom? Are we being selfish for choosing America? Isn't that what the pilgrims did? Looking for freedom and pursuing happiness? If the pilgrim's story became the inspiration to one of the most meaningful holidays in America, why not my story? Why not me?

I remembered wanting nothing more than to become part of this society, because I admired it and because I respected it. I came here to bring what I was, and mix it with what I could become. I just needed a chance. I wanted America to take a chance on me, just like I took it when my family and I decided come here.

I felt so guilty after making my decision to stay here past my March deadline. It felt like I was betraying the trust of the land that took me in, and even worse, I was failing to prove that I was that honest and well intentioned immigrant that I said I was. It did not matter how I felt or who I was, or who took advantage or tricked us, the fact of the matter was that I was undocumented and I could end up paying a high price for my audacity. It did not matter how ashamed of my situation I was or how much I feared getting caught. I was an illegal. The guilt I felt while living in America made me even more timid, but at the same time, with every day I spent here, it also gave me a sense of gratitude that kept me humble and eventually helped me choose my career.

By the end of March I had become paranoid. I thought everybody knew my secret. Anyone in a uniform would make me nervous, especially back then when I couldn't tell the difference between a law enforcement officer and a security guard. Ironically, I was even fearful and would stay clear of fire trucks and ambulances.

One morning, while riding my bicycle to work, I stopped at a big intersection, I could see a police car waiting for his light to turn. I got so nervous that I fumble around getting on my bike and I had the funniest fall of my life. It was nothing big, just dirt and scratches. The police officer was able to see everything and in a split second he turned his lights on, moved his car around and got out to help me up. Meanwhile, I was trying to look cool and pretend it did not happened. The truth is I was not only embarrassed but also so scared of the police that I got up, got on my bike and ran away. I never said thanks or even looked at the officer's face. I do not even think he had the chance to actually help me. I didn't stop to take a look at my leg until I got to work. I was shaking, pale, and feeling heart palpitations. I felt as if I had done something terribly wrong.

I would have liked to thank the officer for his gesture, but what if he asked for my I.D or thought I was here undocumented? Now looking back I can see how wrong I was. For me, those feelings were fruits of my own paranoia and my worst case scenario, but for others like in Arizona, it is an everyday reality. Anyway, like I said…back then I was paranoid; paranoid and ashamed. I am amazed by the fact that I find myself sitting in front of my computer, admitting almost carelessly to everyone that I used to be an illegal, a fact that used to make me feel so guilty and ashamed of myself.

As of this writing, today, ten years and one day after my arrival to America and just one day away from the ceremony where I will be sworn in as an American citizen, I ask you to excuse me and my family for the audacity of choosing America. I can also say that I was right. It was worth the fear, shame, guilt and hard work because when I look in my children's eyes...I feel I bet my life and was rewarded with three beautiful children. I bet on America and I was rewarded with the chance of my life. Regardless of what many people feel and say, I was able to prove once again that the promises of a new life and freedom are still as strong as they have ever been. The United States of America is a country of immigrants, noble, compassionate, worth fighting for and working with, full of opportunities, and is still a beacon of hope for many people around the world… the land of the free and the home of the brave.

CHAPTER FOUR

"As you know, I'm an immigrant. I came over here as an immigrant, and what gave me the opportunities, what made me to be here today, is the open arms of Americans. I have been received. I have been adopted by America."
— Actor and Former Governor of the State of California, Arnold Schwarzenegger.

4.1

Days turned into weeks, weeks turned into months and then tragedy struck on 9-11-2001. Like most of you, I can remember exactly what I was doing. I had just finished washing a car and was on my way to find its owner. While walking through the lobby I noticed there was a commotion around the TV—then I heard an older gentleman say, "We are going to war."

I didn't take him seriously at first. Then I saw the collapse of the first tower. A lady next to me started crying and I remembered staring at the TV for days watching the footage and trying to take it all in. Images flashed of people and emergency workers covered in dust, the American flag at ground zero, the President of the United States on top of the rubble, the firefighters, the search and rescue crews, police officers, the injured civilians, the destroyed streets and businesses, the desperation of wives and husbands looking for their loved ones, the pictures of many faces hanging on a fence. And then came the stories of heroic rescuers and brave heroes.

I suddenly felt anger, sadness, and the frustration of being thousands of miles away and not being able to help. Without knowing, I had my first taste of American patriotism. I was once again in slow motion. I was unaware of the relevance that those acts would have in my own life nor the importance and transcendence of that date. September 11th definitely changed the lives of many people, starting with the victims directly affected by those terrorist attacks, continuing with our domestic relations with foreigners and ending with the lives changed by the emotions of those who simply bore witness.

Pressured by the changes in society around me, like the inability to obtain a driver license and the more detailed backgrounds checks performed by employers, I started to look for alternatives and solutions to my immigration limbo.

I had some Colombian friends with whom I'd become close. We would talk about each other's experiences and in between those conversations I heard for the first time about the political asylum process. Turns out, Colombians are able to apply for political asylum and have had a longer history of dealing with American immigration than Venezuelans. I am considered part of the first large generation of Venezuelan immigrants in the U.S. and as firsts, we have made the way for others based on trials and errors. Because of that trial and error "phase", my parents were very reluctant to take the risk and go through the process. They were as scared and paranoid about everything as I was but they didn't have my desperation or frustration for not being able to continue my education. Obviously they had to think not only for themselves but for the rest of us as a family.

Let me explain. Political asylum is not something to be taken lightly. It is a long and unpredictable process that could mean the end of our immigration problems or just the beginning of a terrible journey that might lead to deportation. With that in mind, my parents carefully and fearfully submitted the application as political refugees. At that time, and without knowing, we were put into another limbo. Many people have the idea that immigration is a first-come/first-serve system. In some cases that is true, but for political refugees that is far from reality. Our asylum process in particular did not have a due date, or an expected day or deadline...it became a waiting game, a test of patience and a tease of frustration. Our saving grace was that while the political asylum took place we were not considered illegal anymore. Keep in mind that an illegal is simply somebody without an immigrant status and while anyone is going through any immigration process, his or her status is "pending", which means no deportation process can be initiated.

The day we received a letter from immigration stating our paperwork was being reviewed was the day I felt I regained my dignity. That was the last time I called myself an illegal. We were finally able to get our own social security numbers and job authorization cards. At the same time my parents submitted the application for political asylum, everybody in the family of working age was able to submit a request for a job authorization card which would allow us to continue to lawfully work in United States. As you can imagine, waiting and waiting became our daily routine. My parents would check the mail every day hoping we would get my dad's letter with the date for the interview with the immigration officer. That letter didn't show up until December 2005.

Honestly, my priority was to be able to fulfill my dream of going to college and continue my education. That was exactly what I did as soon as I had my social security number; register in my local community college. Then waiting for the process to move forward became a little easier. We were able to sustain ourselves without the fear of getting in trouble. I could breathe a little easier; no more fears or paranoia. I was able to study and my parents could change jobs to better themselves. Unfortunately, our papers did not come soon enough for one of my sisters. We were still undocumented by the time Andreina graduated high school, and although she was offered a full ride scholarship for college to study culinary arts, she was not able to accept it due to the lack of "necessary paperwork". For her in particular, life has never been easy.

She was also the one who had the toughest time trying to adapt and learn English. She was a 14 years old sophomore when we arrived here, with no English and only a few friends. She would cry in the afternoons, frustrated by not understanding anything in class, and cry some more in the mornings because she was intimidated by her new and much bigger school. I say much bigger, because our high school in Venezuela only had a total 200 students between seventh and eleventh grade.

Andreina is now married and has a beautiful daughter. She and her husband work hard to provide for their family, but I cannot help but wonder sometimes…how different would her life have been with a college education? Would she have had the same job? Would she have lived with my parents or would she have been able to afford her own apartment?

The differences I see in the outcomes of peoples' lives when given the chance to a better education is not measured in some investigation or documentary. I have simply been able to live it and feel it in my own family. I believe my sister's experience is a definite and tangible example of how immigrants face disadvantages in our society. The differences in how we are prepared to win the battles and challenges we encounter in life are directly related to our level of education.

I truly believe that without education, my chances to succeed in life are greatly jeopardized. A true opportunity to compete in life and enjoy the benefits of your best efforts is only obtainable when you can fully use your potential, in other words, when a child is not left behind and kept from going to school, or when a hardworking father is not condemned to remain static in a fast moving society like ours. As soon as I had the same chances as any other American to compete in life I was able to be part of this society. I began my career, I started a beautiful family and I became an American citizen. I only needed a chance.

Once I had that chance, it was not paranoia and fear that decided how I was to feel that day. It was me and my hard work, me, my skills and my willingness to succeed, me and my perseverance, me and my good luck, me and my desire to give back to this country, my new homeland.

The next eight years where a whirlwind of activity and life. When I think back on all the changes of that time period I am still amazed. I started college in 2003, not knowing what I wanted to be when I grew up. My first major was political science and my first classes were American government and human development, followed by intro to speech and algebra. I also started my own mobile car wash business with my dad.

In 2004 I bought my first house, an unbelievable dream come true at only 23 years old. Then the twin hurricanes Jeanne and Frances destroyed the east coast of Florida, along with my roof shingles, my garage door, and my motorcycle. After all the destruction, I witnessed some of the best of the American people: generosity, compassion, resource management, and leadership at its best. People would donate and share food, clothing, fuel and generators.

Firefighters, National Guardsmen, Police Officers, Coast Guard officials and even lifeguards would work together and volunteer their time giving away MREs, ice and water. Neighbors would check on each other and help with cleaning and shelter. Some people—including my best friend's mother—lost everything due to water damage. The local airport became the command post for Florida Power and Light and every morning you could see people cheering the line of trucks leaving to fix and rebuild light poles and power lines. I remember seeing trucks from other states like Alabama, Louisiana, Texas, Arizona, the Carolinas and even from Canada. The scenes not only reminded me of 9/11 but also inspired me immensely. It was the perfect example of the saying "when life gives you lemons, make lemonade".

What I witnessed in the aftermath of the storms inspired me to change careers, and in 2005 I went to EMT school. I had the privilege of getting to know a great group of firefighters and talented nurses from the local fire departments and hospital. During the summer, I attended the Indian River State College Fire Academy. Shortly after graduating from the academy, I started hunting for a job as a firefighter. In October of that same year, I received one of the best phone calls a firefighter cadet fresh out of school can get, when I was offered a job by a local fire department.

2006 was an eventful year as well. January 6th brought about my dad's immigration interview. Once again we were up for a challenge. After several hours of intense interrogation, tears, reading papers and evaluating evidence, the immigration officer assigned to our case, approved my dad's political asylum case. Three days later I started my new job as a firefighter EMT and in February, Natasha and I got married. The milestones continued and in July we welcomed our first son Victor. By October 2006, I was a firefighter, married with two children and heading back to school. This time, though, I was training to be a paramedic.

In 2007 I had some more small achievements. I finished paramedic school in May and by August I'd became a State certified Paramedic in Florida. By fall 2007, after two months of apprenticeship, I was released to function as a primary paramedic in my department and I celebrated both this and the news that I would be a father once again. My third child, Franco, was born in the spring of 2008. In 2009 I went back to school once more, this time to finish my Associates degree in Emergency Medical Services. Shortly after that I was able to join the Special Operations Team in my Fire Department.

In 2010 I was supposed to walk the stage and receive my associate's degree in a graduation ceremony along with my youngest sister but we couldn't make it due to a scary episode of peritonitis that my mother experienced. That didn't stop our family from celebrating our graduation though; wearing our caps and gowns, we stormed my mother's house and made our own graduation ceremony. I never had a graduation ceremony as funny and loving as that one. All I cared about was being with my family.

2010 also was another important year. On September 29th, two days after my tenth year anniversary of my arrival here in America, I was sworn-in as an American citizen at a small but symbolic ceremony in Palm Beach, followed by a lunch celebration with my loved ones.

2011 brought me my father along with my step mom and my two brothers. They are currently in the process of obtaining their green cards. I also continued to take classes in college, pursuing and finally achieving my dreams of education once again by attaining a Bachelor's degree in Organizational Management. Now I can only speculate about what my future holds. All I know is that I'm extremely grateful for what I have in life. I am aware of how fortunate I am and at the same time I feel obligated to do my part in trying to make my story not an isolated case of tremendous luck but the common and familiar story of many other immigrants.

I believe that with appropriate steps, we can get closer to a more just society in which we are all using our full potential in this competitive and resourceful nation. As I mentioned before, all I wanted was a chance, and when it finally came, I grabbed it and held on tight. Now it's time to help others find their chance.

America, I am not the first and certainly won't be the last to fall in love with you. Not only for who you are now, but because of your humble beginnings. Liberty has been the universal language for many in your land, and justice has always been the calling of your brave. It is for that very reason that, although inspired by noble causes like freedom and justice, I remain vigilant of those who hide behind them to inflict fear and prejudice in our society.

It began years ago, when I first discovered inequity. As my eyes and ears bore witness to people's bigotry, my heart began to pour itself out through words. Those words became phrases, grew into sentences, morphed into paragraphs and finally emerged as an incomplete poem. Without realizing it, I wrote a love letter to America which became the catalyst for change within me, somehow granting me the courage to come forward and tell you who I am, to accept and proudly claim what I am; to stand before you not only as an immigrant, but as a representation of future generations.

Love Letter to America

America, my love, my new love. I've admired you since my childhood and loved you from the moment I first laid eyes on you. You have the richest blend of faces in this world, the largest mix of cultures, and the most amazing land of opportunities. Only you have been a witness to my struggles, my challenges, my achievements, my opportunities, and my disadvantages. I left my homeland behind, my first land, my first flag, my first national anthem, and my first feelings of patriotism. For a while, I felt homeless, damned, and guilty for leaving the only thing I felt mine. Unworthy of my own identity yet trying to adapt and blend in your arms.

Intrigued and mesmerized by your beauty, I wanted to offer you my best, my very best, to obey your laws, to be part of you, to give you something in return, in appreciation for giving my family and me an opportunity to start over. I just fell in love with you, with your first impression, your order, your duties and rights, your flag, your protecting hand... I finally felt safe. I had a new momentum in my life, a force bigger than the fears of this new adventure, a feeling that only a new love could pour in my heart and soul.

Lately I have been troubled by news of old habits. Some that I thought were only part of your history. You, a Motherland to so many other nations, a bastion of equality, freedom and hope. A constant defender of the most vulnerable and helpless. Your stars and bars have always been a symbol of success and pride for so many of your generations. I fear you have allowed people to forget your own struggles, your Civil War and the meaning for our society, the value of your sons' blood in the face of hatred, the importance of your victories for others nations when no one else would extend their helping hands and sacrifice their own blood. You have allowed some to forget your beginnings, the feelings of oppression and injustice, and the true value of your freedom. Some have abused and misplaced the true meaning of patriotism, others, truly believe that they are protecting your essence, when in fact they have inflicted damage to our society now and possibly for generations to come.

Immigrants have been inscribed several times on the pages of your history. Some came by accident, some were brought intentionally, some were forced by their own societies, but most of us have come voluntarily, looking for a better future, looking for you, for what you represent, for the promise of a better life, for the pursuit of happiness.

In your Constitution, you have beautifully acknowledged the importance of equality, freedoms, justice, and the reasons behind such noble causes. Your Constitution inspires with lines that speak to me in motivating poetry, but to others are just an instrument to inflict fear, prejudice, and ignorance. These same people fail to realize in every instance, the longer we have taken to allow immigrants to be part of our society, the deeper the scars in our culture, the wider the gaps that separate us, and the greater the challenges we face in trying to deal with the consequences.

Why have you allowed such social regression in our society? You are the land of the free, the home of the brave, and the example of correctness. You have the courage to stand behind noble and just causes, the beauty of progress, the pride in your sacrifices, the protecting hand for the defenseless, the calm voice of conscience, the serenity of experience, the product of hard work, the dreams of many, and the proof of goodness.

Don't let the asinine ideas of racism allow discrimination against another generation of new blood. Do not let the greed of a few threaten the beauty of your land or the welfare of your people. Do not allow the naïve to be fooled by deception. Protect the children within you, and side always with the very best traits of your culture…ingenuity, compassion, courage, generosity, and justice.

Yours always,
J.G. Monaco.

PART TWO

CHAPTER FIVE

"House Republicans want to pass a strong border
security, illegal immigration bill. We want a bill.
There is no ifs, ands or buts about it."
— Speaker of the United States House of
Representatives, John Boehner.

Every single immigrant,
Hides between his soul and heart
Covered in sweat and tears
A remarkable story of irony,
Where fear and bravery hold hands
Where desperation and hope become one.

There is no doubt that having an immigration debate or conversation is very tough. Immigration is a challenging topic. There are a lot of emotions involved and there are many different perspectives on the issue. I can respect everybody's position on immigration as long as it is respectful and ethical. I may not share the same feelings or opinions, but I can understand and even relate to another's point of view.

Some of the biggest challenges that immigration reform will face here in America will be the wild hearsay by some members of society and the intentional misinformation spread by others. Additional challenges will come in the form of politics, politicians, and special interest groups that will try to cash-in on financial or political capital for their own agendas. My book is not intended for politicians or special interest groups. My book is intended for you, the regular people, those who are the closest to the reality of immigration.

As I mentioned before, hearsay and misinformation play important roles in the challenges that a hypothetical immigration reform will face here in America. In my opinion, the lack of knowledge about immigration and its numerous processes leaves entire communities susceptible to the spread of lies, either premeditated or generated through prejudice, and as consequence, the whole community is vulnerable to becoming fearful or feel threatened by immigrants. In some cases, this can translate into hatred toward other races.

We all know that in some instances, prejudice does not necessarily come from lack of knowledge or understanding, but is a learned behavior. Previous experiences and exposure to varying environments have a lot to do with the way people conduct themselves, and unfortunately racist conducts are no exception. This goes for both immigrants and citizens alike; their opinions are shaped by their own life path. I cannot change anyone's previous experiences, but I can provide a modicum of information about the complicated topic of immigration in the hopes of negating the hearsay. This information is based on my own personal experiences as an immigrant, as well as the preparations my family and I had went through during our immigration process and, finally, my personal investigation into the topic itself.

The other challenge any serious reform will face is the intentional misinformation spread by those driven by a base desire to have others agree with them. For some people, the inability to admit their own ignorance can lead them to intentionally lie to others. They can be motivated by many things; it can be political in nature, be an attempt to avoid being ridiculed or simply to gain popularity. Then there are those members of the discussions who don't necessarily have a particular point of view—and even if they had one, it would be less relevant because their ultimate goal isn't to solve a problem but to take advantage of the situation. Some of those people are politicians wanting to keep their jobs or take someone else's, or special interest groups like the Corrections Corporations of America, ready and very willing to turn a profit from an immigration challenge like ours.

With all this being said, I think there are those who are underrepresented in the current debate, especially those directly affected by immigration laws. An example of this would be the information circulated by foreigners and undocumented people. Though this information is often wrong, it is not malicious. It seems almost harmless when held in contrast to the misinformation given out intentionally to misinform and mislead others by those who are simply racist or are scavengers hoping we never find an effective way to deal with this issue of national interest, yet it can prove just as pivotal to the debate. I can not counter all the wrong "facts" that are out there, but I can address the most common statements and lies I've encountered, those that make up what I call The Myths of Immigration.

Myth I: The Line.

Have you ever heard people saying: "I think they (undocumented people) should go to the back of the line?" Some people also say, "It is not fair for the people that have been waiting in line." Well, the truth is, there is no such line. Immigration is not like the queue for a ride at Disney, nor is it a first-come first-served organization. There are different kinds of immigration status, different kinds of visas and even different kinds of resident aliens. All these degrees of immigration status have their own processes, their own waiting periods, and their own set of challenges. What they don't have is a line.

In my case, I came to America with a B-2 visa, also known as a tourist visa. In order to obtain a tourist visa, my parents had to file a request to petition for a visitor visa and wait for the American Embassy in Venezuela to schedule a date for a visa interview. Most potential visitors or foreigners have to go to an American Embassy abroad and start the process before traveling to the States. Moreover, every American Embassy has different visa wait times for interview appointments and visa processing paperwork depending on their workload and staff availability.

For my family and I back in Venezuela, the wait could have been from six to twelve months before we could see an immigration officer. For other countries the wait could be shorter or even longer. There is also the case of European Union citizens or Canadian citizens—a visa is not required for them to travel to visit the United States as long as they meet certain requirements and follow some additional restrictions, such as being able to visit America for 90 days at a time instead of the 180 days granted to a typical visa holder. As you can see, there is no well defined line or waiting period. It is just the luck of the draw.

The same applies to other immigration processes like political asylum. My political asylum process was long, but uneventful; for others, the process could be fast and loaded with nail-biting deadlines. Or, if the individual is Cuban, they may have their political asylum process automatically approved once they make it onshore. Even if two people submit paperwork to immigration for something as simple as a change of address and their paperwork originates from the same city and at the same time, it doesn't guarantee they will get their paperwork processed at the same time or even in order of arrival.

Myth II: Once an illegal, always an illegal.

Another big misconception is that there is actually a way to become legal after being undocumented or that undocumented people do not become legal because it is convenient for them to remain undocumented. This is a very important point and I want to make sure everybody understands it clearly. Being undocumented is to be in a legal limbo that resembles entering an underground mafia. There is a way in, but not a way out.

Being an undocumented person in America means a lot of things but most importantly, it means that you made a decision that will haunt you for the rest of your life. It is like having a space without a place, a name without a person, a voice without a sound. It is hard to explain but very easy to feel if you are ever in that position. It is a curse that ends only with the birth of your child. I felt it when my son Victor was born. I was already "legal" but I was not what he was. He was and will always be an American citizen.

In truth, I even thought that there were ways to become a documented immigrant. I mean, it had happened for me, so why not for everybody else, right? I was an undocumented immigrant and I was able to apply for political asylum, I was able to marry the woman I fell in love with and my life changed for the better. To say I was shocked when I learned that an undocumented immigrant that crossed the border does not have those opportunities would be an understatement. The difference was in the way we arrived; I initially came to America with an immigration status while they did not.

I was a tourist who became undocumented after my allotted time to stay in America expired. Apparently that isn't so bad. The Mexican or Guatemalan that crosses the border does not enter America with an immigration status, so it no longer matters what they do from that moment on. They will always be undocumented. He or she cannot marry an American citizen nor apply for political asylum. Even if money were no object, they could not even apply for a business visa. As a matter of fact, an undocumented immigrant cannot even claim a winning lottery ticket. They are a nobody, not even a placeholder in society, trapped in limbo, nonexistent in the eyes of the government, an illegal.

Undocumented immigrants that crossed the Mexican border fleeing hunger, lack of opportunities, and in some cases certain death have no way of becoming lawful persons, and have no chance to gain immigrant status. The only option they have is to return to where they came from and hope that American authorities in their countries do not have records of them violating America's immigration laws. You see, it is a felony to cross the border illegally and that felony could ban that person from coming to America for up to ten years according to the Illegal Immigration Reform and Immigrant Responsibility Act of 1996.

As I discovered this information, it made me wonder...what is the difference between crossing the border or using a raft to come to America? What is the difference between a Cuban and a Haitian? Is there one? Why, if we trust Cubans or Venezuelans to become part of our society and serve our communities as policemen, firefighters, and even serve our country in our armed forces, are we so skeptical of others that seemed to come with the same desires and aspirations? Haven't we all come to America for the pursuit of happiness? Aren't they all risking their lives just to have a chance to start over?

If you're not sure what I mean, let me explain. The United States allows citizens from Venezuela and Cuba (two of the most outspoken anti-American governments in the western hemisphere) to come to America and become part of our societies with less skepticism and prejudice. On the other hand, we have Mexico, our neighbor and business partner, never hostile towards American people, and a great contributor to our workforce and culture. Mexico is also key in our geopolitics, often serving as the lynchpin in global debates. Politically speaking, when America does not have Mexico as an ally, we usually find it harder to influence and even to get along with the rest of Latin America. Mexican authorities have acted on numerous occasions as mediators in Central and South American conflicts, conflicts that can be tied directly to our national interest and even our national security. Yet these immigrants are treated as if they are sub-par. Why?

The way I see it, if we cannot solve our own immigration issue with our neighbor Mexico, how do we expect to lead a mediation between Palestinians and Israelis with respect to Gaza? Or help with the troubles between Pakistan and India? How influential can we actually be to the rest of the world if our own "house" is a mess?

Without a doubt, it is in our best national and security interest to be able to secure our borders, to protect our citizens from drug cartels' violence, our children from human trafficking, our teenagers from drugs in our streets, and our society from the cowardly hands of terrorism. But it does not stop there. It is also in our best interest to enhance and regain the leadership role in the world, and since immigration is not a challenge exclusively reserved for Americans, how we address the issue will most likely be used as a reference point by many other nations. Today, The United States of America is an—depending on our future actions—will most likely remain an inspiration for many around the world.

I can't help but feel lucky now that I know the difficult road others face. I know I was fortunate and will always appreciate the opportunity given to me by this country to be part of this society, to contribute to this nation, and to raise my children in a safe environment. I just would like others to have the same chance I had, an opportunity to prove themselves. I would like others to succeed, to grow, to be safe, to live in peace, to contribute, to be free, to stop being afraid, to have fewer limitations, and, most of all, contribute their strength to America.

Myth III: The Anchor Baby.

There is a belief that pregnant Mexican women cross the border just in time to give their babies the American citizenship they need to reside legally here in America. Some believe having a child that is an American citizen will keep them from being deported back to Mexico. It won't.

According with the Illegal Immigration Reform and Immigrant Responsibility Act of 1996, deportation procedures apply to any person unlawfully present here in United States. This includes sick people, the elderly, minors, pregnant women, workers, felons, and even new moms. Anyone who is undocumented could be subject to deportation if found unlawfully present in United States. I can see how some people could think that a minor U.S citizen has the right to have his mother with him at all times, even if that mother committed the crime of crossing the border to come to America. U.S citizenship is obviously highly regarded in our minds, but in this case, being an American child doesn't allow your mother to stay with you if she is undocumented. You can stay, but she'll have to go.

The reality of this myth is quite harsh. If an undocumented Mexican mother is found here by a federal agency like ICE, she will be deported —with or without her children. The undocumented mother is given three options: take her American children back to Mexico with her, leave her American children in America with documented family members or friends, or as a last resort, leave her American children with the Department of Children and Families.

Based on human nature, on what I think even my own mother would do, I believe that most Mexican women would take their children back to Mexico with them. Fewer would leave them here in America with family members, often because women are reluctant to return after a deportation procedure; they do not want to go through the trauma of crossing the border again. And I'd be willing to bet that a mother leaving her children under DCF's care is a rare event.

An American citizen can petition for his parents to become legal residents in United States, but he or she has to be over 21 years of age. In fact, according to the official immigration website (*http://www.uscis.gov*), the American citizen has to be over 21 years of age, file a form I-130 and provide proof that the person he is petitioning for is indeed his father or mother. Then, as I mentioned before, it is almost impossible to predict how long will the process take and/or what the ultimate results of the petition process might be.

This is just the start of the process. A process which, by the way, I believe is organized and necessary. After the initial steps, there are some additional forms to be filed and deadlines that need to be met before a parent is finally able to receive his or her permanent resident alien card (a.k.a green card). So, no American child can petition for his parents until he turns 21 years of age and furthermore, undocumented women are subject to deportation regardless of being mothers of an American born child. This doesn't seem like a very solid plan for gaining citizenship.

Finally, the notion that somehow expectant women cross the border just to give birth in America then wait for their child to be 21 years old to apply for a green card is so far from reality that it almost becomes comical. Once again, is just a misconception that sadly enough, even some politically influential people have been repeating as a truth. Crossing the border, crossing the Atlantic Ocean, swimming across Rio Grande, hiding deep inside cargo boats, or going through the dangers of any other method of coming to America illegally is not easy, is not safe, and is not that appealing. The journey to come to America is a sacrifice. It is the last resort, and the only alternative in the face of hunger and danger, the price of freedom for some and the price of hope for others. The road to America has become the final resting place for many souls that paid the ultimate price for their pursuit of happiness. It is the biggest challenge that rewards with the chance for a better life. I do not doubt that there have been some pregnant women that dare to cross the border for a better life, but I also wonder how bad life must be to force a woman to make such a decision.

Myth IV: Freeloaders.

There are a lot of negative words used in our communities when referring to immigrants, but one of the most frustrating is when they are labeled freeloaders. The notion that undocumented people live off the government handouts alone, that they come to America for all the welfare benefits of this great nation and take from the natural-born citizens is rampant and couldn't be further from the truth.

I always thought my parents were hard workers. While in Venezuela, I remember my dad going to work after taking us to school and then not coming back home until very late at night. He looked tired, he smelled like metal, he always carried receipts and other papers, a suitcase and a plastic bag with some groceries and fruits for everybody at home. Yet, somehow he managed to look professional until the very last minute before his night shower. His shirt was occasionally dirty but always tucked in place, his blue jeans looked weathered but always above the waistline and his shoes were occasionally dusty but always tied as well.

My mother was not much different. Although she switched from a working mom to a stay-home mom, her jobs were much like any other job. She was my dad's unofficial secretary, customer service representative, and logistics director at the same time. That never kept my mother from being there for the children and together, my parents were the biggest example of hard work and dedication that I had while growing up.

Nothing compares to what my whole family had to experience after moving to America though. As I mentioned before, I thought my parents were hard workers, until I saw my dad after his first day of work here in America. That day, my dad went from being a "hard worker" to "the hardest worker in the history of mankind", at least to me. After that first day of work, my dad came home looking like I'd never seen him before. He was sunburned, he had dirt on his face, his clothes were ruined, he was still wet from all his sweat, his hands were beaten and cut, his finger nails were black, and he smell like gasoline and soap. His facial expression alone expressed how hard and hot it was to spend the entire day cleaning cars under the hot Florida sun.

To this date, my dad still washes cars, but now he owns his car detailing business. I still see him tired, dirty and wearing his weathered clothes at the end of a hard day at work. When things get tough at my job, I look up and thank God for giving me the chance to have the job that I have, and hope for the day that I do not have to see my dad work so hard to be able to provide for his family. The idea that someone might call that man a freeloader is honestly infuriating. Freeloaders are those who are so lazy that they refuse to work, not because they aren't capable, but because of a greedy and slothful nature—none of which applies to my father.

The truth is, nearly any immigrant you come across is an example of hard work. I don't say this from a place of personal bias, but because that is actually what they are known for. They are hired because they are willing to perform difficult, demanding, undesirable jobs with less than appealing benefits (if any). For this hard labor, they earn lower wages than any other demographic in our country.

Some people think about immigrants as freeloaders because of the welfare benefits they sometime get and not necessarily because they believe immigrants are lazy or slothful. So the real issue is actually underlying the immigration issue; the truth is that what some people believe immigrants take away from our country, the so-called benefits they enjoy for being poor in our generous society, is another debate entirely, one of social welfare rather than immigration. The problem is that these issues have become clouded, Those people who do not see immigrants as a real and functioning part of our society, begin to resent their receiving basic assistance for food or shelter. Some of them even feel that immigrants—documented or not—do not belong here and therefore should not receive any of the benefits of our welfare system.

There is the added problem of, well, society problems. Every society has a smattering of undesirable members, criminal elements and those who try to game the system and get something for nothing. No matter how many honest, hard working immigrants someone encounters, a single story of an undesirable committing fraud or causing mayhem can cloud the judgment of thousands—especially if the story is spread across the internet.

My fear is that the longer we keep immigrants segregated within our own system, the longer it will take us to get over our differences and the bigger the scars of such segregation will be. As I mentioned before, immigrants are synonymous with hard work and labor in many circles, and their sheer numbers make them a very real portion of our society. While some may think that immigrants take more from our system than they put in, my research found that in most cases, immigrants give more to our society than they actually take out.

For example, a recent study titled Immigrants in Arizona: Fiscal and Economic Impacts was conducted by Judith Gans, from the Udall Center for Studies in Public Policy (at the University of Arizona), found that, "Immigrants in Arizona generated a net 2004 fiscal contribution of about $940 million toward services such as public safety, libraries, road maintenance, and other areas". The study estimated that the total state tax revenue from immigrant workers was about $2.4 billion in comparison to the fiscal costs of 1.4 billion for education, health care, law enforcement and other services, leaving approximately one billion dollars in revenue for the state of Arizona.

Another study from the College of Business Administration of the University of Nebraska at Omaha prepared by Christopher S. Decker, Associate Professor of the Department of Economics and Real Estate, found that in terms of government cost, the immigrant population in Nebraska accounted for $144.78 million from food stamps, public assistance, health, and educational expenditures in 2006. At the same time, the state's immigrant population contributed about $154 million in the form of property, income, sales, and gasoline tax revenue in 2006, which gave immigrants a "contribution to cost ratio" of 1.07, indicating that this group pays in about 7 percent more than what it uses in terms of governmental support.

It doesn't end there. John Kasarda and James Johnson, Jr. from The Kenan-Flagler Business School of the University of North Carolina found that Hispanics contribute about $756 million annually in taxes while costing the state of North Carolina about $817 million in education, health care, and corrections. However, the study states "The net cost to the state budget must be seen in the broader context of the aggregate benefits Hispanics bring to the state's economy". Given that Hispanics have a spending impact of approx. $9.2 billion on the state's economy and (according to the study) without Hispanic labor, for example, the state's construction industry output would likely be considerably lower, the impacts are further reaching than just those two numbers. For example, the state's total private-sector wage bill could be as much as $1.9 billion higher without the immigrants.

The reports and studies that I have cited here were chosen because of their impartiality and because they were prepared and performed by reputable Universities. These institutions do not posses the hidden political agendas or biased opinions that other organizations have, and furthermore, I favor the use of Universities' studies because they are most likely based on the facts of the investigations, hard work, and dedication of their authors.

From the findings of my research, I can comfortably state that freeloader is a term that has been falsely and unjustly related to immigrants. It is another myth that aims only to fuel the animosity that exists towards the immigrant population of our country. It is a lie that has become a truth only because it has been repeated; don't fall victim to it.

CHAPTER SIX

"THE SEPARATION OF FAMILIES TO ME IS VERY CLOSE TO MY HEART BECAUSE WE LIVED THAT AS IMMIGRANTS. I STRONGLY FEEL THAT WE ARE ALL CONNECTED, AND HAVING FELT PEOPLES LOVE AND SUPPORT FIRST HAND THROUGH DIFFICULT MOMENT IN MY LIFE, MAKES ME FEEL IT'S OUR RESPONSIBILITY TO HELP ONE ANOTHER"
— SINGER, SONG WRITER AND ENTREPRENEUR, GLORIA ESTEFAN

6.1

This is the story of Abel, a hard working immigrant and friend of mine who bravely shared the story of his trip from Pinal Del Rio in Cuba to America.

I was sitting in the backyard when Abel approached me. Abel has a certain character that makes him unique. He's around five feet nine inches tall and weighs about one hundred and eighty pounds. He has black wavy hair, brown droopy eyes, his skin is toasted from the Florida sun and his hands show the scars of the hard labor he's done since he was a child back in Cuba. On that particular afternoon, he offered me a plate of typical Cuban food; puerco and arroz con gris (pork and rice with beans). As we sat enjoying the meal, he said it was his first time cooking in la caja China (the Chinese box), a whole pork cooked inside a metal box, with the charcoal not on the bottom as I've known but on top of the box. It is definitely a different way to cook pork, but let me tell you—it works.

In between great food and a couple of beers, Abel and I started a conversation about his job, his day to day routine, and so on. I learned of his passion for bees, his knowledge about farm animals and working the land. He talked to me about the children he left behind, his house, his parents and his friends. Unlike most Cubans I have talked to, Abel had a relatively easier life in Cuba. He lived in a rural town, away from the drama of the capital. His skills raising bees and collecting pure honey made him famous in his town. At one point he was able to care for about 70 beehives. He used to sell a one liter bottle of honey for the equivalent of $0.50. Because of the extra income, he was able to buy and sell farm animals and afford luxuries that were inaccessible for others. More importantly, by living in a low profile area he could also stay away from any spotlight of the Cuban government. However, that spotlight eventually found its way to his town. In just a few weeks, the Cuban government managed to dismantle his farm. They confiscated all the honey, bees, and farm animals. They also threatened him with jail, fines, and other serious consequences if he continued to profit from his farm.

Although it was pretty interesting to hear his tales about the bees and animals, I was more interested in hearing about his "D-Day"—the day of the crossing, his new beginning, his "new birthday", a day that every immigrant has in his past; the day he came to America. Slowly and tactfully I steered the conversation towards that day. I started hinting to him about how hard it must have been to leave it all behind, and even how difficult the actual journey must have been. A smile, a stare, a sigh, and a couple of seconds in silence made me realize I just opened his Pandora's Box. I was not disappointed by what he had to say. His story was in many ways, so very similar to everyone else's and at the same time, unique and personal.

Abel's arrival in America was recent, only about five years prior. The most amazing part of his story is not what he has accomplished in those first five years, but how he actually managed to leave the island of Cuba.

6.2

Before getting to the story, Abel got up, got us each a fresh beer and started talking about a man, his contact in America. The contact was a man with a high speed boat, which would be Abel's ticket to freedom. Soon I realized that in this story there were a lot of players. There is Abel, the man with the "ticket" to freedom, his friends, and all the strangers united by their common desperation to escape the tyranny of the Cuban authorities and the fear and hunger that marked their daily lives. In order to do so, they would have to trick the American Coast Guard and last but not least, cross the 90 miles of sea that separate two completely different worlds.

The man with the boat (we'll call him the Captain) called Abel to make the final arrangements for the trip. They discussed the details in more specifics; the numbers of Cubans leaving the island, the day, and the location, but did not discuss price. Money was not to be mentioned over the phone. Everything was tense and the call was quick. The clandestine nature of the deal left no place for manners, contracts, or any type of formal business transactions.

It wasn't long before a problem arose: the Captain wanted to transport 30 Cubans in his boat, but Abel only wanted 15. Each extra passenger meant more money for the Captain. Abel explained the pricing structure and I was amazed. I found out that if you have a child that can sit on your lap he only pays half of the fee and babies on arms do not pay at all. I could not help but think about my three children having to go through such trip. Believe it or not, it wasn't this risk that limited the number of people fleeing the country. Everybody wants to go to America, but not everybody has ten thousand dollars to pay for his trip or has someone in America who could pay the fee for them.

For Abel, though, the less people with him the better, since it meant less chances of getting caught by either Cuban or American authorities. The boat owners don't have to fear Cuban authorities as much as they have to fear the American Coast Guard. The inflatable boats that Cuban authorities have are no match to the human traffickers 30+ foot long boats, however, the risk of getting caught by the American Coast Guard is greater. This means profits have to be enticing enough for the Captain to make the trip. Aware of the increased danger with each additional passenger, Abel stuck to his number; the Captain stuck to his and Abel hung up the phone without a deal.

There was no rush—he could continue his life and wait for the proper time and a safer trip. A week later, another Captain called him, asking for the same 30 people. Abel refused again and no deal was reached. Finally a third captain called him and agreed with Abel's proposed 15-person trip. The date of departure was set and the only thing left to do was to get the people together. The surprising fact was that money was never talked about while all this was being planned. As a passenger, it is on you to know the costs and make arrangements in advance for who will pay for your trip once you're in America.

Three days later, it was time to go. In the middle of the night 14 people huddled in the back of an old dump truck, covered with sheets and blankets as they wove down dirt roads and across shortcuts to get out of the town. They were minutes away from freedom, with the beach at a visible distance, when a random police checkpoint appeared in the middle of the street. Abel was sitting on the passenger side of the truck and the driver could see how nervous he was getting; he begged him not to do anything rash. Abel let his hand rest on his homemade machete. He felt as if his eyes were about to pop out of his face and he could feel his heart pounding in his throat. He tightened his jaw and started breathing heavy. The guards stopped the truck and asked the driver for identification papers. Shortly after that, their worst fears came true— another guard spotted the people in the back of the truck. They were ordered to come out. Abel knew it was over; the guards would take them all to jail and they would become just another forgotten bunch of prisoners added to the long list of Cubans who lost everything because they reached for freedom.

What Abel didn't know was that the guards had another plan in mind. Knowing that human trafficking means money, they gave in to their greed and decided to try to work a deal with Abel. If he paid them, he and his friends could pass. Abel refused to pay, though, and so they were ordered to stay put by the guards. At that moment, fear took hold of everybody and without any advanced planning, they all ran in different directions, heading into the woods.

According to Abel, everybody made it back to their homes without any major incidents. The next day, Abel got a phone call from a family member telling him the police were looking for him. As you may have heard, nothing is secret in Cuba. It is a society that rewards whistle blowers, especially those who expose others that want to leave Cuba, or dislike the government, or just speak out about democracy and freedom.

Now it was Abel who made the call. It was that night or never, regardless of numbers. With no goodbyes to his children (a ten year old boy and an eleven year old girl), no hugs to his family, not a kiss to his loved ones, and no blessing from his parents, he had to go. Abel got his driver friend and found the 30 people "ready" to leave that same night. They started picking them up and by the end of the afternoon they had everybody on the back of the truck once again. This time they made it to the beach and the waiting game started. Abel got on top of the mangroves and started calling the boat with his cell phone.

Without noticing, they had picked a place really close to a Cuban Coast Guard post, so close they could hear them talking. By sunset, the situation started getting hard to manage especially for the children. If you have spent any time in the mangroves at night, I am sure you have experienced the wrath of mosquitoes and sand flees. The women had to keep their children from making any noise so everybody got in the water and tried to stay as quiet as possible. The boat was scheduled to show up around 8 p.m.; it was passed midnight and the boat had not shown up yet.

Being so close to the Cuban Coast Guard kept Abel from signaling the incoming boat, which had gotten lost off the Cuban shore. Sometime after midnight Abel was finally able to guide them to their spot. The boat, a 37 footer with three outboard engines and two people on board, finally made it. Quickly and quietly, women and children started boarding, then the rest of the men. That was when they discovered another problem—there weren't 30 people, they were 34. Four extra found out about the "freedom boat" and followed them into the mangroves. The boat captain did not want to take them and a small but very intense argument erupted. At the end, 34 souls made it onto the boat and with that, 36 people total got ready to leave Cuba behind.

Right when they started the engines, two inflatable boats with six Cuban guards on each one of them showed up and blocked their exit. The guards demanded everyone to get out and for the captain to surrender the boat. The captain and his crew member were well armed but no match for the twelve guards as they went back and forth between threats and insults.The children started crying and the women started yelling, the guards started getting more anxious, and before anybody could realize it, the captain made a move. He opened the throttle wide and the tip of the boat went up in the air. The waves created by the momentum of the boat were so big that both Cuban boats rocked from side to side and most of the twelve guards fell in the water.

The feelings were indescribable: excitement, sadness, anxiousness, euphoria, tears and smiles. All 36 souls made it out of Cuban waters. In total, 9 women, 6 children and 19 men left Cuba that night in search of a better future and the freedom they so desperately needed.

The journey didn't stop there. The captain of the boat steered them towards the Gulf of Mexico and shut the engines off, he lighted a cigar and took a break. He made a list with everybody's names and contact information in America. After that, he resumed the trip. Their final destination was the Florida Keys.

About 15 minutes later, already in American waters, the boat ran out of gas. The Captain started calling on the radio to see if any fishing boat in the area could give him enough fuel to make it back to the Keys but there was no answer. Finally, just after dawn, the Captain made contact with a fishing boat whose staff knew him. The fishing boat only had a few gallons of fuel to spare—just enough to make it about two miles—so they decided to tow the floundering boat the rest of the way to Florida. The rope had to be long enough, just in case the American Coast Guard showed up so they could cut the rope and deny any relation with the smugglers. So, just like that, the unnamed crew of a passing boat towed the boat full of fugitives until they could see land.

While the conversation was going on, I could not stop thinking about the fact that we were talking about people, not goats or pigs or bees but people; men, women, and children desperate to leave. As a father, I honestly don't know what I would do. Damned by my life that put me there, and having to choose between allowing my children to be brainwashed by a tyrannical and obsolete system and to grow in poverty and misery, or to jeopardize the life of my biggest treasure and gamble with my future. What would be courageous—to stay and keep my loved ones with certainty and the predictable or leave and risk so much? What would be stronger—the fear of communism or the fear of losing a loved one in those 90 miles?

Abel continued his tale, explaining that, as planned, the Captain fired up the outboard engines about a mile away from shore. The boat headed towards the beach at full speed. They approached fast and crash landed on the sand of the Florida Keys. All they had to do now was to stay put, wait a couple of hours to give enough time for the boat to leave and then find someone that could dial 911. From there, they would be taken into the custody of American authorities, who would confirm their identities and open a clear path to citizenship, which is automatically provided to those fleeing Cuba.

At the end of Abel's story I was stunned. I felt humbled by his honesty and moved by his traumatic past. I told him I admired his courage and the determination he'd shown during his trip to America. When I told him his story should be in the papers, he smiled at me as if I was being naïve thinking that his story was unique. He pointed to an older lady and said, "Do you see that lady there?"

I nodded, looking closer at the woman. She was well into her sixties and short, only about five feet tall.

"She is my aunt,"Abel said. "She almost lost her life for not knowing how to swim. The boat that was supposed to pick her up didn't wait for her and left her in the middle of waves. People in desperation trampled her in order to get to the boat and she was pushed down in the water".

Then Abel turned back to me, his expression sad. "I also have an uncle that lost his wife when they were coming here".

He told me about the tragedy, explaining that the boat his aunt and uncle were coming on was spotted by the Coast Guard. The speedboat was so heavy that it flipped over when it hit the waves created by the fast approaching Coast Guard boat. The Coast Guard also shot out the engines of the speeding boat. People panicked when the boat flipped and attempted to get out of the sinking boat. In the end, everybody ended up in the water. The refugees were desperately trying to get on the Coast Guard boat. There were not enough ropes to get everybody out of the water. Somehow his uncle made it safely onto the Coast Guard boat. As he searched, he discovered that his wife was not one of the frantic people trying to get to safety—she never made it out of the sinking boat.

Abel's uncle tried to jump back into the water, determined to find her, but he was stopped by the Coast Guards. I could only imagine the horror he felt as Abel described the scene; the desperate husband screaming, pulling, and pushing as he tried to make the officers understand that his wife was sinking with the boat, the inability to help her. After breaking somebody's nose, Abel's uncle was able to get free from the guards and he dove back into the water. He was alone when he pulled his wife's body out of the sinking wreckage.

I asked Abel if his uncle was also at the barbeque, but he just shook his head. The man was repatriated to the Communist Republic of Cuba three days after his catastrophic arrival in the US. To make things worse, he wasn't allowed to see his wife after the day of the tragedy. Ironically, her body was made an American citizen, in just seven days, in order to be buried in Miami as requested by her family in Florida.

Every story I heard had a meaning to me. Not too long before that night, while working my shift at my fire station, I responded to a call where a vehicle was slowly submerging in a pond. A witness at the scene stated it looked like the person inside was not conscious and slowly went under water. Two of my brother firefighters jumped in the water in an attempt to find the car and rescue whoever was inside. Twenty minutes later, they found the car, opened the driver's side door and recovered the body of a middle aged woman. I will never forget her face and especially the frustration I felt for not being able to save her life. With that feeling of frustration in my mind, I could not even begin to imagine what that husband must have felt while trying to explain in Spanish to the American Coast Guard that his wife was still under water, that he needed to jump, that he could not stand by while his wife drowned, and that he actually needed help.

This Cuban tale is not some plot from a movie; it is a true story, though I've changed the names to protect the privacy of my friend and the safety of his family, both those here in America as well as those back in communist Cuba. Abel's story, his aunt's tale, and the sad account of his uncle should give you a unique view of the challenges that we currently face with regard to immigration. These stories highlight the unique nature of the debate, illustrating that not everything is black or white. Immigration is not just about a vague argument over laws or the lack of laws, but it is about people. People with stories of hardship and courage who are willing to risk it all on nothing more than hopes and dreams. It is about individuals who come to our shores for a myriad of reasons, but who are nearly all overwhelmed by feelings of appreciation and gratitude; it is also about the feelings of patriotism and skepticism that most American citizens find within themselves.

Immigration is worthy of a serious debate, but that debate must be based on respect and understanding. We must acknowledge that immigrants can—and do—encompass traits that are desirable additions to our society; they bring modesty and appreciation, intelligence and creativity, integrity and honesty.

CHAPTER SEVEN

"REMEMBER, REMEMBER ALWAYS, THAT ALL OF US, AND YOU AND I ESPECIALLY, ARE DESCENDED FROM IMMIGRANTS AND REVOLUTIONISTS"
— FORMER PRESIDENT OF UNITED STATES, FRANKLIN D. ROOSEVELT.

One of the things that I have noticed in recent years, and honestly a large part of the reasons why I decided to write this book, is that there are some misconceptions about what it means to travel or migrate to the United States. I have talked to native-born Americans that didn't know the difference between an American issued Visa and an American passport. I have also met with people that seemed surprised that I was a permanent resident but did not have an American passport. Some were even surprised by the fact that it took me ten years to become an American citizen. Its obvious that many of us do not understand the complicated process of immigration, though we understand the importance of it. I personally believe that it is an honor to be an American citizen or to be any other citizen for that matter. Most immigrants are very aware of the feelings of ownership that citizens show toward their homeland.

That is the reason why most of us proudly show the flags of our home country wherever we go and that is why we tend to strike up a conversation when somebody speaks our language or has our same accent. If you do not believe me, ask any member of the military how proud they are to show their American flags on their left shoulders when they land in foreign lands and when they help other nations recover from natural disasters or even when we have occupied other countries. At the same time, it is understandable to see foreigners with flags on their hats from Canada, England, or Haiti. It is called patriotism.

Patriotism is not exclusively for Americans or Venezuelans. Patriotism is the love and respect anybody shows to the land they come from, whether it is a land of big mountains or desolated deserts, a developed and strong nation like ours or a little island in the last corner of the world. Expressing love for where we originated doesn't exclude love for where we find ourselves now, and it doesn't indicate an approval of the reigning government or political parties in our homeland. It merely shows that we honor our roots. Immigrants should always be tactful and respectful of the country that welcomes them; Americans should always be tactful and respectful of the country that allows its citizens to leave them to become part of us.

Citizenship is granted in most countries of the world to all people born within its borders. If you are born in Venezuela you are a Venezuelan citizen. If you are born in America, under the 14th amendment of the constitution of United States of America, you are an American citizen. As a citizen, you are able to enjoy the benefits and responsibilities of being American. You can enjoy the safety of the due process, the right to vote, freedom of speech, a true balance of powers, the right to obtain an American passport (which is the most recognized identification document for anybody in or outside of United States), and for the vast majority of Americans, other perks that we do not think much about like safe infrastructure, public services, free enterprise, education, health, no food shortages or struggles to find water, professional police officers and firefighters. In just a simple word: progress.

For some citizens of foreign countries wanting to come to America, the process starts with obtaining an American visa. A visa is basically a legal authorization to enter the United States which has been granted by our embassies abroad. There are two main categories of American visas; which one you are issued depends on the purpose of your travel. Nonimmigrant Visas are issued for travel to the United States temporarily while Immigrant Visas are issued to travel to United States with the intention of permanently living here.

There are some instances where a foreign citizen does not need an American visa to travel to America. For example, countries in the European Union are not required to obtain an American visa to visit the United States as tourists, but they are only allowed to remain in the States for a period no longer than three months. So, an Italian citizen that wants to come to America only has to obtain an Italian passport and fly into an airport of his choice here in America. Then he can stay up to three months before he goes back to Italy. For a Colombian citizen, though, it is quite different. He would have to obtain a visa through an American embassy (typically located in the capital of the country), then he would be allowed to fly into the United States, where he would be able to stay up to six months.

While researching the types of Nonimmigrant Visas for temporary visitors, I found that the number of visas that existed far exceeded the number I expected to find. In fact, I found 32 initial categories in which somebody could qualify for a visa. Here is a brief overview of those categories.

Categories and Types of Visas

Category	Visa Type
Athletes (competing for prize money only)	B-1
Au Pairs (International students working/nannies)	J
Border Crossing Card: Mexico	BCC
Business Visitor	B-1
Diplomats and Foreign Government Officials	A
Domestic Employees (accompanied by Employer	B-1
Employees of a designated International Organization	G1-G5, NATO
Foreign nationals with extraordinary abilities	O
Free trade agreements (Chile, Singapore)	H-1B1
Medical Treatment, Visitors	B-2
Media, Journalists	I
NAFTA Professional Workers (Canada, Mexico)	TN/TD
Religious workers	R
Students	F, M
Tourism, Vacation, Pleasure	B-2

Some of these visas have prerequisites which must be met before they can even be applied for at the American embassy. One example is that teachers, professors and scholars have to have a "Program Approval" entered in the Student and Exchange Visitor Information System (SEVIS). Another example is that the Department of Homeland Security (DHS) and the United States Citizenship and Immigration Services (USCIS) must approve a Form I-129 petition, filed by the U. S employer for any visitor with extraordinary abilities in science, arts, education, business or athletics, and a form I-914 if the visitor wants his immediate family members to travel to America.

If that all sounds tedious, complicated, and time consuming, its because it is. Sure, some of these processes are fast and effective, but others are old and obsolete. If you look back at the table with the visa types, you will find a visa for temporary workers. I asked myself, why isn't that type of visa resolving a large portion of the immigration problem by allowing seasonal workers to come temporarily to the United States? A little researched was all it took to turn up the answer. First of all, the U.S employer (a company here in America) must obtain foreign labor certification from the U.S Department of Labor and then DHS and USCIS must approve a form I-129. Once those steps have been reached, an applicant or prospective worker can apply for the H-2B. I can't help but wonder how many farm owners are willing to go through all the paperwork processes every time they needed a farm worker on their farms. Furthermore, I don't know many farm workers with the capacity to make contact with an American farm owner and convince him that he is the ideal candidate to fill the position. Its quite obvious that the process to obtain various types of visas is not adapted to the needs and reality of today's society.

It is important to mention that some visa processes have been and still are effective in achieving the results expected from them. For example, athletes and their managers find it a little easier to deal with USCIS. Business visitors are also some of the more fortunate applicants and have better chances of success when dealing with immigration. Yet for other processes, we have a long way to go to reach any sort of efficiency.

There is another category of Visa, the Immigrant Visas, which we haven't discussed. These visas are for foreign nationals who want to live permanently in the United States. Immigrant Visas also vary in how they are handled, where they are applied for, and how long it takes to obtain them.

Generally speaking, to immigrate to the United States with the intention of staying permanently, a foreign citizen has to be sponsored by either a U.S citizen relative, a permanent resident (green card holder) or by a prospective employer. First, an I-130 Petition to USCIS has to be filed by the sponsor then the visa can be requested.

After this petition has been approved by USCIS, the National Visa Center (NVC) takes over. This "new" entity will serve as the link between the sponsor here in America and the petitioner abroad. Here is an example of how the process works: if an American citizen goes overseas and decides he or she wants to marry somebody from a foreign country, they would need to apply for a visa for the prospective spouse. First they would have to get married, complying with all legal requirements for both the United States and the foreign country. Once they are married, the American citizen has to file a I-130 Petition for Alien Relative. After the petition has been approved, the NVC takes it and finishes the process. There is also a Diversity Visa Program in which visas are provided to citizens of countries with low rates of immigration to the U.S., though this is obviously a much less common route to citizenship.

Trying to get an estimated time for the completion of this process is almost impossible. In fact, anyone looking for information on the official website (http://travel.state.gov) will find that it actually states: "Many approved immigrant petitioners take additional time because they are in numerically limited categories. The length of time varies from case to case according to its circumstances, and cannot be predicted for individual cases with any accuracy…"

The type of Immigrant Visas also varies depending on what kind of immigrant or relative is petitioned. There are two main categories of Immigrant Visas; those that are numerically limited, and those that are not. Numerically limited means that only a specific amount of visas are issued in a year. These visas are issued for more distant relatives and for certain employment situations. The other category of Immigrant Visas deals with visas that do not have a limitation in the number of applicants per year that are allowed to enter the United States. This is the category where wives, fiancés(e) and others immediate relatives are found. The different types of Immigrant Visas can lead to quite a varied processing time—for example, the spouse of a U.S citizen's petition generally takes less time to process and be accepted than a petition for the parents of a U.S citizen.

Is important to note that a visa is the first legal status that an immigrant can obtain here in United States. The immigration process does not stop there, though. As you know, Nonimmigrant Visas allow foreign citizens to travel to the States for business, education, or pleasure. The Immigrant Visas allow foreign citizens to come to the States to live permanently. Almost all visas have expiration dates, where some can be renewed and others do not allow for renewal. For those with the option of renewal, there are other complications. With every renewal comes another set of paperwork. It also requires, in most cases, another background check (including fingerprinting), additional fees, and more waiting periods.

Each immigrant hoping to relocate to the US will need to obtain a visa which allows them to become a Lawful Permanent Resident (LPR) of the United States of America. Changing their status from a visa holder to a LPR starts with filing another form or petition (I-485), submitting to another background check, and in some cases involves face to face interviews. Obtaining the status of LPR is an important step towards the final process, or as I call it the ultimate goal. With every change of status comes reassurance that your new life is indeed here in United States. For many immigrants this translates into stability, serenity, and the confidence needed to continue establishing and adapting life in their new home country: America.

You might not know this, but an immigrant who has achieved LPR status is commonly known as a green card holder. This title refers to their paperwork, which simply states that somebody can stay and live in United States as long as their Resident Card (green card) is valid or active. Green Cards also have expiration dates. Some expire in two years and others in ten years. After three years as a Permanent Resident some are eligible to apply for citizenship (e.g., in the cases of marriage), though for others it could take up to five years to be eligible for citizenship (e.g., in the cases of political asylum).

The process of citizenship is a lot easier, faster, and less stressful than the process for obtaining a visa. It starts with filing another form (the N-400), paying a fee, submitting to another background check, attending an interview, and finally taking an oral test performed in English and based on a group of 100 questions about very basic American history, politics, and other general knowledge questions. At the end there is a "Swearing ceremony" in which you officially become an American citizen.

Citizenship is the ultimate goal of most immigrants. I am sure I am not the only one that felt honored when granted American citizenship. It is the final chapter between you and the American immigration system. I remember my green card being taken away from me as soon as I walked into my citizenship ceremony. I was so reluctant to give it away that the immigration officer had to walked me through the motions.

"It's OK," he said. "You don't need it anymore. You are a citizen now".

It meant a lot to me. It was a liberating, exciting, proud, and emotional moment in my life. Everyone
experiences it in a very personal and particular way. I believe we could all agree it is a good feeling knowing that we are now truly equals and we can all call this land "our homeland."

As you can see, when a foreign citizen wants to come to America, there are quite a few steps to take. They will have to see if they need to fulfill any prerequisites before applying for a visa, then they apply for the visa that is appropriate and hope it provides the ability to become a LPR. Finally, after some time, they could become an American citizen. The process is long but necessary. All those steps, all the paperwork, waiting periods, fees, background checks, medical examinations, interviews, and then more paperwork made me appreciate my citizenship that much more. More importantly, this process is the first line of defense from serious threats to our security and stability. Our embassies play a crucial role in sorting and selecting the best possible candidates for a chance to visit, work, study or live in United States of America.

During my path to citizenship, I think I have experienced every possible emotions and state of mind that exists. I was fingerprinted five times, had several pictures taken, paid a fair amount of fees, and I had a lot of waiting time. But at the end it was all worthwhile. I truly believe that, like me, the vast majority of immigrants would do it all over again even knowing what they have to go through. It might be hard for a current citizen to imagine, but immigrants—particularly undocumented immigrants—would give almost anything to have the chance to go through a process that although long, costly, and tedious, will take them out of that legal limbo and guarantee one of this country's most important and humbling tenets: that all men are created equal.

There is so much information about each and every one of these immigration processes that it is virtually impossible for me to share it all without writing two or three more books. I've summarized as best I can, but I encourage you to investigate, read, or even just take the time to glance through as much information about immigration as you can. I guarantee you will be surprised, but you will also be educated. You will learn to sort the true statements from the false flags, the real issues from the fake but most importantly you will have the ability to form your own opinion on this matter, without the influence of hate, without the drama, without the speculations, and it will be as factual as possible. I recommend the websites: *http://www.uscis.gov* and *http://www.travel.state.gov*.

CHAPTER EIGHT

"A SIMPLE WAY TO TAKE MEASURE OF A COUNTRY IS TO LOOK AT HOW MANY WANT IN.. AND HOW MANY WANT OUT" —
FORMER BRITISH PRIME MINISTER, TONY BLAIR.

It is impossible to write about the current immigration debate and not discuss the infamous Arizona Law (AL). This law isn't included because I believe it has actually something useful or meaningful to offer in the search for solutions to this challenging topic. On the contrary, its heinous nature and defeasible wording present evidence of how an unscrupulous special interest group has been able to influence politics, and how politicians have been able to deceive the public.

If you believe that the AL is a piece of legislation that improves the lives of people and solves—or at least helps with solving—the immigration challenge we face in today's society, I am afraid you are sadly mistaken. Many who believe this legislation is the answer are either part of an industry that stands to benefit from the law (e.g., the Corrections Corporation of America) or are part of the larger group which has been effectively deceived by political rhetoric. Few have actually read the AL and even fewer understand its implications.

The AL consists only of a few amendments to the Arizona Statutes; amendments to four chapters and five sections to be specific, a total of sixteen pages. The solution to Arizona's immigration problem, according to Arizona State Senator Russell Pearce and Arizona State Governor Jan Brewer, exists only in those sixteen pages of Senate Bill 1070. Just to make a simple comparison, as of this writing, the Arizona Statutes covering cosmetology consists of fourteen pages. I find it difficult to believe that a comprehensive approach to illegal immigration can be achieved with only a few more rules than those required for someone who will be working in a beauty salon.

Over the next few pages, we will explore how the AL came about. I will actually quote parts of the amendments as I will try to explain its implications in our day to day lives; while I won't hide my distaste for the amendment, I will allow you to judge it for yourself. The analysis begins with a story run by Laura Sullivan, a highly decorated National Public Radio (NPR) News investigative correspondent.

The report, which was published on the NPR website on October 28th, 2010, shared the tale of the city manager of Benson, Arizona, a man by the name of Glenn Nichols and his exposure of a behind-the-scenes effort to draft, and pass the new immigration law. Nichols claimed he was approached by two men who offered him an opportunity to build a prison for women and children who were detained because they were illegal immigrants. The men promised that the prison would have a positive impact on his community due to the amount of revenue it would bring from each prisoner on a daily rate.

After Nichols came forward, NPR spent several months analyzing hundreds of pages of campaign finance reports, lobbying documents, and corporate records and found a quiet and behind-the-scenes effort by the private prison industry to draft and pass the AL. During this investigation by NPR, Arizona state Sen. Russell Pearce claimed the bill was his idea but instead of pitching it on the floor of the Arizona state house, he apparently took his idea to a group in Washington D.C called American Legislative Exchange Council or ALEC.

According to NPR's investigation, ALEC is a membership organization comprised of state legislators, corporations and associations like the tobacco company Reynolds American Inc, ExxonMobil, the National Rifle Association and last but not least the billion-dollar organization known as Corrections Corporation of America (CCA). CCA is the largest private prison company in the United States. Four months after that meeting in Washington DC, the model legislation became the Arizona legislation that we know of today.

I am not going to go into details about ALEC, or the technicalities of lobbying or the significance of this organization; it is important enough to simply highlight that the AL was not a bill created by the people, for the people. It is instead a bill created by corporations, for corporations that manipulates our fears and our passions, pitting our feelings of patriotism against our feelings of compassion, confusing our convictions with our duties and for what? For nothing more than a profitable bottom line.

In my opinion, the AL is not a law, but rather a grotesque and repulsive handbook on how to harass those who cannot defend themselves. It is a half-baked approach to immigration and is not even efficient for remedying the problems faced by the people of Arizona. It is a law that was created and drafted with the intention of benefiting the multimillion dollar private prison industry, not for helping you, nor me, nor the victims of human trafficking. It is the government allowing the corporations and special interest groups higher standing than the people who elected them.

Most disturbing of all are the consequences of not only its creation but its implementation. The AL is a passionate topic for most of us, and passion being the outburst of overpowering emotions, it allows the distancing of logic and reason from the discussion. With emotions in control, the topic becomes divisive; with the public divided, the corporations and special interest groups are free to continue profiting without worry. It forces us to take steps backwards and weakens the true spirit of America.

The AL seems to be pulled out of the darkest pages of history, when men, women, and children were nothing more than assets for a corporation and when many were persecuted for their color of their skin, race, creed, or nationality. It promotes the idea that some members of our population are more valuable than others; it reverts our society to a history that some of us would like to forget—and which others would like to resurrect, not because they believe it is right, but because they believe it will stimulate their personal financial growth.

Now that we can see the origin point for Arizona's misguided law, let's take a closer look at the most controversial portions.

> *SENATE BILL 1070*
> *Article 8. Enforcement or Immigration laws*
> *11-1051. Cooperation and assistance in enforcement of immigration laws; indemnification*
>
> *B. For any lawful contact made by a law enforcement official or agency of this state of county, city, town or other political subdivision of this state where reasonable suspicion exists that the person is an alien who is unlawfully present in the United States, a reasonable attempt shall be made, when practicable, to determine the immigration status of the person. The person's immigration status shall be verified with the federal government pursuant to 8 United States code section 1373(c).*

This is one of the aspects of the law that has generated the most controversy. It is evident that the law flirts with legalizing racial profiling based on the fact that police officers will have to established and use certain criteria to determine who is an alien first and then if the alien is lawful or unlawfully present in the United States. Racial profiling is simply the assumption of knowing or predicting somebody's race.

Because of how recent and painful the issue of race was and in some cases still is, racial profiling is outlawed in our country. On the federal level, racial profiling is challenged by two major pieces of legislation— the Fourth Amendment of the U.S. Constitution which guarantees the right to be safe from search and seizure without a warrant, and the Fourteenth Amendment, which requires that all citizens be treated equally under the law. Racial profiling, by its very nature, leads to differential treatments and relations with people depending on how they look and what we assume they are. In the case of the Arizona legislation, it could lead to discrimination and the assumption that somebody (most likely a Latino) is an immigrant or worse, an illegal immigrant. The problem is that America's face changes with every new generation. Because we are a nation that was created and built on a foundation of immigration, every generation is more mixed, and the assumption that Americans are of a certain race becomes more and more obsolete.

The best example is within my own family. One of my children has green eyes, another has coloring much darker, and the oldest looks completely different than the others. In other words, if you were to spot them walking down the street, it would be impossible to predict with any accuracy which of our children is an American citizen and which is not. The melting-pot history of our country ensures that, the more time that passes, the more difficult it will become to determine origin or genetic history with a simple visual inspection.

Yet under their new law, an American citizen could be held in jail under the assumption that he or she is an immigrant until they are able to prove that he or she is lawfully living in Arizona. In America, due process establishes the entitlement of a citizen to proper legal procedures. One of them is the principle that a person is presumed to be innocent until proven guilty in a court of law. This concept is being trampled by the AL when it suggests that a person that looks like an immigrant has to be detained until determined that he is "legal".

It would be the equivalent of ordering the suspect in a murder investigation to remain in jail until the police decide to actually charge them with the crime. As far as I know, anybody under police questioning has the right to leave at any time, unless that person is under arrest. Furthermore, in order to be under arrest, the suspect has to have charges brought up against him and that is only after sufficient evidence has been collected. If at any time, the state attorney or police department violates any of the suspect's rights, the prosecutors run the risk of losing the case altogether. This isn't the case in Arizona; there, you can be detained without reason and without charge until the officials decide if they will charge you with a crime.

It is important that you, the reader, understand that the main reason I disagree with the Arizona legislation is because of my feelings of compassion for others. Perhaps it is because I was there once; I know how it feels to fear the police, what it means to be nothing, to be in limbo, unable to show who I really was and what I had to offer. Secondly, as an American citizen, my concern is that my own constitutional rights will be violated because of how I look.

Ask yourself this: if you would never have to prove your American citizenship to a police officer, why should someone else? Why should I

—an American citizen like you—have to prove my citizenship to a police officer or run the risk of being sent to jail indefinitely until my status could be confirmed, simply because I have dark hair, dark eyes or dark skin? Doesn't this violate the very tenets our country was founded upon?

SENATE BILL 1070 continues…

F. Except as provided in federal law, officials or agencies of this state and counties, cities, towns and other political subdivisions of this state may not be prohibited or in any way be restricted from sending, receiving or maintaining information relating to the immigration status of any individual or exchanging that information with any other federal, state or local government entity for the following purposes:

1. Determining eligibility for any public benefit, service or license provided by any federal, state or other political subdivision of this state.

Is education considered a public benefit? If so then a ten year old girl, undocumented, who was brought here by her parents is unable to attend school. Does this seem like it is in the best interest of anyone? What about classes to learn English? Because of the vague wording of this legislation, the public benefits brought into question surpass what many might suspect. What about help after natural disasters—does it mean that if the house of an undocumented immigrant gets destroyed by a hurricane, he or she is condemned to die under rubble rather than have the public service of rescue by firefighters? What if there are children living there; what if those children are American citizens? What about in the case of an epidemic where vaccinations are given by the government for the people infected? Do we deny immigrants the vaccines? Do we save only the legal children but not the illegal? What if they are siblings? What about a major catastrophe like a radiation leak where evacuation is needed and performed by the government? Do we evacuate only American citizens to different states?

Unfortunately, these are legitimate questions raised not only by compassionate people, but by those who understand the broad scope of the law as it is written. If ever a rule brought the true meaning of "All people are created equal" into question, this would be it. Any concerned

American citizen should understand that this half-baked law is ineffective, destructive and actually presents more difficulties than it resolves.

SENATE BILL 1070 continues…

13-1509 Trespassing by illegal aliens; assessment; exception; classification

A. In addition to any violation of federal law, a person is guilty of trespassing if the person is both:
    1. Present on any public or private land in this state.
    2. In violation of 8 United States code section 1304(e) or 1306(a).

Everywhere and nowhere; those are the words that come to mind when thinking about this section of the bill. Nowhere is where illegal immigrants can live or go to rest after harvesting the food we eat, or fixing roofs that protect our houses, or collecting the garbage from our driveways, or helping us raise our children. Everywhere is the word that comes to mind when thinking about illegal immigrants and where they will be subject to persecutions and discrimination.

Under this section of the law, an undocumented immigrant is consider trespassing if present on any public or private land in the state of Arizona. That includes parks, restaurants, gas stations, schools, groceries store, etc.

I wonder, would that allow the owner of a restaurant to deny entry to an illegal immigrant because he or she is (according to the AL) a trespasser? Would I have to show my American passport before sitting down to dine? Will there be signs in the window explaining that service is only provided to whites, not to those of Spanish or Mexican descent? Where do we draw the line to prevent such acts?

To me, this section highlights precisely why I believe the AL is a step backward in our society. It makes us look and feel as if we were in the times of pre-civil rights-movement. In fact, if read carefully, it opens the door to inappropriate past conducts and behaviors that American society has worked so hard to overcome through time, education, and a lot of sacrifices.

SENATE BILL 1070 continues…

C. A person who is sentenced pursuant to this section is not eligible for suspension or commutation of sentence or release on any basis until the sentence imposed is served.

I recently went to a public meeting in Stuart, Florida. The meeting was about immigration, with the goal of informing the public about the intentions of several Republican State Representatives to bring an Arizona-style legislation to the Sunshine State. It was hosted by a non profit organization named Consensus and the only guest speaker was the Republican Florida State Representative for district 82, William D. Snyder. In this meeting, Rep. Snyder was asked, "Is holding somebody in jail without setting a bond an infringement of his Due Process?" Rep. Snyder's answer, blunt and defiant, was a simple "Yes." If you're wondering how he excused this violation, so are we; without explaining or expanding on the subject, he just continued to the next question.

I have a hard time believing a man that has no problem admitting that his proposal is clearly violating somebody's right, and at the same time, claims that his proposal is necessary to defend the constitution. So, for those who call themselves protectors of the constitution I would say this: It is a very difficult task to defend and protect the constitution from close-minded people, from those near-sighted individuals that pretend the constitution of the United States of America is there for the benefit of an elite few, and from those who intend to pass or alter legislation in order to fund their own personal bank account. I hope that it is clear that the Arizona law—and all laws modeled after it—legitimizes the creation of a group of second class residents that will only hurt our society for generations to come.

SENATE BILL 1070 continues…

13-2319. Smuggling; classification; definitions

A…
B. A violation of this section is a class 4 felony.
C…
D…
E. Notwithstanding any other law, a peace officer may lawfully stop any person who is operation a motor vehicle if the officer has reasonable suspicion to believe the person is in violation of any civil traffic law and this section.
F. For the purpose of this section:
 1…
 2. "Procurement of transportation" means any participation in or facilitation of transportation and includes:
 (a) Providing property that facilitate transportation including travel arrangement services or money transmission services.
 (b)…
 3. "Smuggling of human beings" means the transportation, procurement of transportation or use of property or real property by a person or an entity that knows or has reason to know that the person or persons transported or to be transported are not United States citizens, permanent resident aliens or persons otherwise lawfully in this state or have attempted to enter, entered or remained in the United States in violation of law.

In this chapter, I have purposely omitted some parts of the law, not because it is convenient for me, but simply because in some cases these parts are not relevant and in others they are just common sense statements. This isn't the case with section 13-2319. The troubling part of this section is the impact it could have with regular citizens.

My parents go to church every Sunday, as I'm sure many of you do. Before going to church they sometimes borrow a 15 passenger caravan and pick up children who want to go to church but have parents who cannot drive them for various reasons. This is a common practice in our area; many churches even have their own vans which they send out. Some of the parents may be working, some may not have a car and others may not have a driver's license.

Potentially, some of these families might be living in United States without documents. The most important and remarkable thing is that these children want to go to church and learn about faith and Christian values. My parents are doing it because they believe its the right thing to do. After reading the law, I asked myself if this wording meant my parents could be charged with human trafficking for driving undocumented children to church. What about two friends who carpool to work? What about having a party at your house and having people that may be undocumented attend? Suddenly the scope of the law became terrifying; essentially, it requires Americans profile those they associate with or face consequences. Is this law truly effective? Does it really help immigration or just serve as a façade for persecution?

With this kind of legislation, some people could be subject to unfair or unjust treatment by local law enforcement agencies or even state police departments. As an American citizen and a firefighter, I am aware of the professionalism of our law enforcement agencies and their ethical responsibilities in our communities. I essentially trust their judgment at the time of determining the differences between a legitimate human trafficking call and a van with people going to church. With that said, my concern is for the few that could use this kind of legislation as a tool to harass and persecute minorities in our country.

SENATE BILL 1070 continues…

13-2928. Unlawful stopping to hire and pick up passengers for work; unlawful application, solicitation or employment; classification; definitions

A… (It is unlawful for a person to stop to hire someone on the street).
B… (It is unlawful to a person to enter a vehicle in order to be hired).
C… (It is unlawful for an undocumented immigrant to apply for a job, solicit work or perform work).

As you can see, in this section of the law there is not much to explain. It is self explanatory, yet still surprising that once again the AL managed to go after a certain demographic in our society.

13-2929. Unlawful transporting, moving, concealing, harboring or shielding of unlawful aliens; vehicle impoundment; classification),
A. It is unlawful for a person who is in violation of a criminal offense to:
 1. Transport or move or attempt to transport or move an alien in this state in a means of transportation if the person knows or recklessly disregards the fact that the alien has come to, has entered or remains in the United States in violation of law.
 2. Conceal, harbor or shield or attempt to conceal, harbor or shield an alien from detection in any place in this state, including any building or any means of transportation, if the person knows or recklessly disregards the fact that the alien has come to , has entered or remains in the United States in violation of law.

There is again the dilemma about what to do with undocumented people. What happens if one of my family members is illegal? Is this law asking me to turn my own family in? I cannot live with them, drive with them, work with them, and cannot be with them at all without breaking the law? As terrible as it sounds, and as much as I hate to draw the comparison, I believe that this must have been how people felt under Nazi Germany when they began passing laws governing Jews. Was it not a crime at that time to conceal, harbor, shield or attempt to conceal, harbor or shield a Jew without reporting him or her or the entire family to the Nazi authorities? Like I said, I personally do not like to compare such an evil and dark part of global history with our own current events, but at some point we have to stop turning a blind eye to what is happening and stand for what we believe is right, honest, and just.

The rest of the AL focuses on the employers that knowingly and/or intentionally employ undocumented immigrants. It also describes the consequences and penalties for doing so, including license suspension and/or the revocation of work permits. And finally it states how the attorney general could follow up on complaints made by a concerned citizen about a company that employs unlawful workers.

8.4

The Arizona legislation is a law that was created to benefit the private prison industry. It was poorly written by corporate attorneys with blatant disregard for the American constitution. It is a cancer that will divide and weaken our country. It undermines the rights of American citizens. It does not provide answer to our challenges. It degrades the image of America with our neighbors, and most importantly, it does not represent the values and principles conveyed through our own pledge of allegiance, which lists us as "One nation, under God, indivisible, with liberty and justice for all."

Sadly enough, the state of Florida, as well as others states around the nation are considering passing similar laws. In the Sunshine State for example, there are alarming similarities with Arizona's political situation. It has its players that start with Governor Rick Scott and his plan to make Florida a "business friendly" state (funny, coming from the man that was the CEO of the company that had to pay $1.7 billion in Medicare fraud). There is also Florida State Representative William D. Snyder (elected as Martin County Sheriff in 2012), and last but not least the Correction Corporation of America, Management Training Corp, and the GEO group.

Then State Rep. Snyder introduced a bill in August 2010, just after the AL debate was gaining momentum. That bill is, according to his own words: "pretty similar to the one passed by the Arizona legislature." Also according to Snyder's own words, he is being more careful in how he handles the bill. In Snyder's opinion, the reason why the AL is being challenged and has such a hard time being implemented is because it was not "worded adequately".

This left the State of Florida with a state representative running for sheriff that was determined at the very least to benefit from all the media exposure of the immigration debate in Florida, Special interest groups (CCA. Mgmt. Training Corp, GEO group) that are very well connected to the highest level of government in the state of Florida and a governor that is shockingly in favor of the privatization of the prison system.

I was not joking or trying to be overly dramatic with my statement about the Arizona law being a "cancer" in our society. It is already beginning to spread and it is far from benign. Because of all the arguments, differences, hate, divisiveness, and potential profits to special interest groups that it represents I have to say that the citizens of America should unite and stand against not just the Arizona legislation, but any law modeled after it.

PART THREE

CHAPTER NINE

"As I would learn later on, developed countries will always welcome the Einsteins of this world -- those individuals whose talents are already recognized and deemed to have value. This welcome doesn't usually extend to the poor and uneducated people seeking to enter the country. But the truth, supported by the facts of history and the richness of immigrant contribution to America's distinction in the world, is that the most entrepreneurial, innovative, motivated citizen is the one who has been given an opportunity and wants to repay the debt."
— Alfredo Quinones-Hinojosa, "Becoming Dr. Q: My Journey from Migrant Farm Worker to Brain Surgeon"

Not too long ago, I was introduced to Paola, a young woman with two children trying to start fresh in life once again. I invited Paola to my home for dinner and I took the opportunity to talk to her about her story as an immigrant. I wasn't sure what to expect from her tale. She has been here in America for a while, and she speaks very good English. Both her children seemed pretty well adapted; they showed good manners, they were respectful, and obedient to their mother. Paola has a beautiful round face, brown eyes and long, wavy, dark brown hair which she wore pulled up into a pony tail. Her skin was much like mine, a light brown that seemed like the permanent tan House Speaker Boehner strives to achieve.

Paola was eager to start telling me her story as soon as we finished dinner. I started the conversation by explaining the topic of my book and I gave her a quick summary of my written chapters along with a hint of what future chapters were going to be like. Then I started asking about her tale.

Paola is 33 years old, mother of two boys—Hector, the oldest, is 14 and Samuel is 9. Paola was born in Mexico to a large family, child number 15 of 16, and by the time she was 18 years old all but one of her siblings have moved to America.
After high school, Paola got married and had her first child. At 19 years old, she was a married woman, mother of a son, living at her parents, taking care of her ill mother, raising her son and two nieces, and working the fields where her family would get their food for the year.

Paola still described her family life as uneventful even though she lost three siblings due to illnesses and tragic accidents in Mexico (Paola never actually met them). She also knew about hard labor from early age and her family have been divided due to migration ever since she could remember. Unfortunately for Paola, her marriage did not last long.

Shortly after her baby boy was born she divorced her husband. After the divorce, her relationship with her ex-husband took a turn for the worse and she started fearing for her and her son's safety. Still, she remained in her parents' house caring for her mother and the house duties without any intention of leaving her home. For her, leaving her parents' house was not only unnecessary but dangerous. She had and still has a special bond with her parents, heightened since she is the baby girl of the family and was the last of the children living with them.

The situation with her ex-husband worsened rapidly. He had a hard time letting go, he had control issues and to make matters worse he was becoming more physically and verbally abusive toward her and even his own son. She had a hard time thinking about the possibility of leaving her parents' house. She could not imagine her mother without her, or herself without her mother for that matter. Who would care for her mother, harvest the fields, and who would keep up with their house?

She finally had to make the decision to leave after her ex-husband threatened taking her son away from her. For the first time in her life, she felt her home was no longer safe and with that, she was able to get enough strength to ask for help.

One of her brothers, Raul, offered to help her. He told her she could stay in his house in Florida. A week later, that same brother was in Mexico and ready to drive her to the U.S-Mexican border. Paola did not have any kind of papers or visas to come to America. As a non-college graduate, unemployed, without big savings, and now a single mother, there was no visa she could apply for and her only chance was to "cross", as Mexicans usually refer to migrating to America.

At 20 years old, a very young and naïve Paola had to choose between the risk of staying home in a domestic violence scenario or the risk of taking her one year old son across the Rio Grande and through the American desert. She had to choose between the relative "safety" of certainty and the uncertainty of the unknown, the known risks of staying home and the unknown risks of crossing the border.

Paola was incredibly calm while telling me her story. I personally could not wait to hear how she crossed, how hard it was, or how she made it. It was not easy to follow her story because she would go back and forth between different days and characters. I tried to keep her focused in her story and slowly tried to keep up with all the details she was giving me.

9.2

Her last day at her parents' house was gloomy, and there was neither farewell party nor celebration. Her mother knew her only help was about to leave. Paola felt overwhelmed by feelings of guilt, sadness and fear. She had seen how others had made the same decision, but she had never put herself in their shoes. For the first time, she was able to understand why tears instead of smiles, why fear instead of hope, and why sadness instead of excitement. Paola grew up thinking immigrating to America was exciting for those fortunate enough to "cross".

Little did she know as a child, that her siblings immigrated to America; not because of excitement, but need; not for partying, but hunger; not for wealth, but safety. Paola explained that, as a little girl, her idea of America was that of a country with the most intelligent people, advanced enough to stop the rain just with a magical machine that would always protect the crops. I suppose as a farmer, she would see all the hard work being washed away by massive rain or dried out by the droughts and think to herself, "this would not happen in America". For her, America was bigger and better, and the place that many of her own family lived but where she never thought she would go. That was the reason behind all her feelings of fear, hope, sadness and excitement. For immigrants, there is a combination of the sadness of leaving loved ones mingled with the excitement of arriving in America, all mixed with the fear of the unknown and the hope of a new beginning.

Paola left her parents' house in the dark. They drove all night, all day the next day and all through the following night to finally make it to a little town near the border early in the morning. There, they stayed in a roadside motel, a place where finding a person to help them cross the border (known as a Coyote) was not that difficult at all. It seems like in every town around the US-Mexico border there are people knowledgeable about the land, the short cuts, the easier passages, and all the contacts they need in order to successfully make it into American territory.

That service is obviously not free but definitely cheaper than the trip Abel made from Cuba to Key West on a speedboat. Coyotes are typically Mexicans citizens; they get paid in cash, most of the time in Mexican pesos, and typically they do not act by themselves. They usually have a contact here in America, or a person that would help him accommodate his immigrants until they are ready to be sent or picked up by relatives. In some cases, immigrants without money or people to look for them are forced to work in what is known as the modern version of slavery before being dropped somewhere, becoming instantly homeless.

Coyotes are also typically young, and the younger they are the more reckless they behave. Some of them are there just to steal money from crossing immigrants, and they prey on young women by committing rapes and kidnappings. Older coyotes tend to be more conscientious about what they are doing. They are also more experienced and have better chances of getting across the border without being caught by American Border Patrol officers.

For Paola, getting a good coyote was crucial. She was not walking alone as she was responsible for her 16 month old son and a young teenage cousin. She also met other people at the motel wanting to cross like her, and soon that same day they became a group of 11 people. Her brother Raul wanted to stay there until he could find the right person to get them across, so they rested that first night. The next day, Raul made contact with an older man willing to take them all across. After negotiating the cost and the places they were going to meet once in America, the Coyote set a time to start the walk later that same night.

When it was time, the Coyote parked outside in the parking lot of the motel and knocked on the door. Raul did not open the door as he had a bad feeling about that coyote. He told the rest of the group that they could go with that coyote if they wanted, and since the only person who seemed to know something about the border was Paola's brother, they let him be in "charge" and did not question his instincts. The reality was that they were all lost, without any idea how to cross. In fact, not all of them were even from Mexico—several of them were from Guatemala. After several minutes waiting outside, the Coyote got back in his car and left.

The next day, Raul tried again. This time he negotiated crossing the border with a much younger man. This Coyote was not by himself, he had sort of a "wingman". This wingman was an American citizen, a "Güero", as Mexicans typically refer to a blonde, white American.

Once again, the time to start walking was set for later that same night. Paola only packed some water, powdered milk and a few snacks. She only had a few diapers left, she did not have extra clothes for herself or the baby, nor any blankets or towels. There was not a single first aid kit or even the most basic survival kit. It must have been either complete improvisation or pure ignorance and inexperience, either way, Paola was risking way more than what she was aware.

They started walking as scheduled with this second Coyote. They trekked all through the night and by sunrise they were at the Rio Grande, the natural border between the State of Texas and Mexico. Paola mentioned that the walk was uneventful. She had to carry her son through the whole night; luckily for her, baby Hector slept most of the way. Carrying his weight, however, was clearly no easy task.

Every time Paola would mention what she'd done, I would turn around and look at my own children. I would ask myself if I would—or could—do the same. I wondered if I had the courage or the will to walk all night with my son or daughter on my shoulders. I could not and still cannot answer that question, I just hope I am never forced to make such decision.

Early in the morning they rested by the river. She was able to eat some of her snacks and make a bottle for her son Hector. She told me that at the Rio Grande, there were people that helped everybody get across. They had a rope that went from the Mexican side to the American side which made it a lot easier for a non-swimmer like Paola.

Crossing the Rio Grande was the first taste of danger Paola had to get through. She went to the edge of the river and tightened her backpack. She secured Hector with her right arm and then she grabbed the rope to cross the river with the other hand. Slowly, Paola got herself in the murky water where some of the other people were already crossing or getting ready to cross. She could feel the river current but she could not see anything. With the cold water up to her shoulders, she tried to keep Hector's clothes dry by raising him as high as she could, but it was too difficult. Between caring him and grabbing the rope it was hard to even keep herself balanced. Finally, she made it to the safety of the other bank.

Once on the other side, Paola's clothes were drenched with water and so were little Hector's. After about an hour, all 11 people made it across the river. The Coyote was trying to convince Paola that she should take her clothes off and let them dry. Paola said she was subject to constant harassment by both the Coyote and the Güero. The looks, the suggestions, the inappropriate comments and jokes and even the constant attempts to physically touch her, forced Paola into a continuous state of alert.

As they continued to walk north, they arrived at the first town on the American side. It was the middle of the afternoon and already exhaustion was setting in. Their clothes were still wet, everybody was hungry, thirsty, and tired. The Coyote got a room in a motel where the whole group was going to stay for the night—or at least that is what Paola thought. Some took showers, some ate, some drank and some just rested. The only time the Coyote stayed with them was while walking. The rest of the time, he and the güero would try to stay as far as possible from the group.

By midnight, the Coyote was knocking on their door and ready to start the walk again. From this point on, the walking had to be done more carefully. They were already in American territory and people were more hostile. Their final destination was El Paso; from there; they could all take buses to go pretty much anywhere in the United States.

So it began, another night of walking with a baby on her shoulders. Paola did not pack extra clothes for her or baby Hector and with 11 people in the room, she did not feel comfortable taking her clothes off to let them dry. She was only able to do change and dry Hector's clothes while they waited in the motel room.

Her feet were swollen from walking on uncomfortable shoes, her knees where also hurting from walking, and her back was terribly sore from carrying the weight of her baby and her backpack. It did not matter. There was nothing that could stop Paola from making it to El Paso—

except of course, American Border Patrol officers. After walking almost all night, the entire group stumbled right into an Immigration raid. To that point, Paola hadn't really thought about the estimated 50-50 odds she had against her. Mexicans think there is a 50% chance of crossing the border without being detained by the American Border Patrol. She thought, like many young people do, "that will never happen to me".

The Border Patrol detained everyone that day and night. They were booked in the system, given water and then their nationalities had to be verified before deportation orders were issued. The next day, they were mixed with other immigrants and ICE (Immigration and Custom Enforcement) police drove them in buses back to the Mexican-American border. There, American Border Patrol officers unshackled them and made them walk once again. This time though, towards Mexican territory.

I asked her how the Border Patrol officers were. I wanted to know how she was treated, and if they caught the Coyote. About Border Patrol, she said "they were very nice", respectful and professional. There was no mistreatment, abuse or harassment to her or to anybody in her group. She told me nobody talked about the Coyote, as he pretended to be one in the group of twelve and nobody turned him in.

The güero, on the other hand, was not taken by ICE. He was taken into custody by another agency. Border Patrol officers told Paola that her group members were lucky because the güero was presumed to be responsible for the death of several immigrants while crossing the border. Police had not been able to prove it, but told her he'd also served in prisons for rapes, assaults, batteries, possession and robbery. For Paola, now she not only had to fear her ex-husband, but also the coyotes and "cholos", criminals who thrive around the border by dealing in drugs and weapons.

9.4

Paola walked back to Mexico. She could see all the vehicles driving the opposite way towards the United States and others driving towards Mexico. At the Mexican border they were met by Mexican immigration authorities and she was surprised that nothing was said or asked other than "Welcome to Mexico". Paola wanted to go back to the same town where she'd begun the odyssey but she wanted to do it without her brother's help. After her recent experiences, she thought she'd do a better job at finding another coyote; in fact, she wanted the rejected Coyote who'd been her brother's first choice.

So she went to the same town and set out looking for the Coyote. Once back in town, she actually had some time to buy food, diapers, and more water. As I mentioned before, finding a coyote was not hard to do. The town was very small and in one of the stores she visited, she saw the man she was looking for. This time, the Coyote wanted half of the money up front and the other half once they were free to go in America. She agreed and so did the other five remaining people. Later that night, the Coyote began to lead the 8 remaining immigrants on their journey once again.

As before, the walk was fast paced with very little time to stop and rest despite the very tough terrain. Sometime after midnight, Hector started getting restless. He cried several times through the night and finally she asked to stop to check on her son. Hector was bundle up pretty tightly, but soon after she started uncovering him, she discovered that he was running a high fever. He was not sweating, was hot to the touch, and moving constantly. Nothing would calm him down, and she did not have anything with her to lower his fever. Staying there was not an option, as it wouldn't help his condition. There was nothing she could do other than try to console him as they moved on.

The rest of the night was tense. The Coyote did not want the baby to cry and give up their location. Besides, with every cry, Paola's nerves were getting more and more out of control. Cholos around the area know that behind every child that crosses the border there is a desperate mother and they know exactly how to exploit that. Paola took her drinking water and dampened some clothes to put on Hector's head in a desperate and futile effort to stop or even lower the fever.

They made it to the Rio Grande before dawn. Still dark out, this time they made it to a different part of the river, where there was no rope to help her get to the other side and no people waiting to help them onto dry land. To make matters worse, Hector's fever was not cooling down even with the wet clothing she was putting on his head. The water felt even colder and the current was faster. This time the water was up to her neck and the darkness of the night made her feel like she was in the middle of a nightmare, a feeling that was heightened when, as she entered the water, Hector screamed like the water was breaking his little body.

What do you do when your children have fever? Who do you look for? How do you comfort them? In moments of others need, sickness or tragedy, I always compare it with my own life. How lucky I am to have a roof over my head, and the medicine that cools my children's fever, or the ability to seek help if my daughter needs a breathing treatment.

I could not help but think that one night, while I was probably sleeping on my bed, Paola was crossing the Rio Grande with her son burning with fever and screaming in pain as she struggled, her mouth barely above the water. That night while many of us were dreaming, she thought she might be living her worst nightmare; dropping her son at any time into the fast moving, cold, and murky water. She could not feel her legs. Her arms were shaking from effort, the muscles on the verge of giving up from exhaustion while mine were warm and covered with a clean sheet. She was cold, shivering, and she could not see much in the dark while I was dry and still…asleep on my bed.

The current took her several feet downstream, making crossing the river longer and harder. Seconds felt like minutes, those minutes felt like hours and those hours felt endless. When she finally made it to the other side of the Rio Grande, her emotions took over and she gave in to frustration, fear, and the adrenaline rush of not only almost losing her own life but her son's. Hector was quiet and still as if knowing that it was now mom's turn to cry. She saw his face, touched him, kissed him, and caressed him. Hector was just watching her, in silence, just staring at her face.

That was a special moment between Paola and her baby boy, when they both thanked God for giving them each other. Paola needed the strength to keep going and not give up that only comes from the eyes of your child. Hector needed the warm touch of his mother when his body was aching and burning in fever.

The Coyote was getting impatient and he told Paola he was going to carry the baby so she could walk faster—and so he did. The coyote's pace was even faster than before. Paola was having a hard time keeping up with him, and he started getting ahead more and more until Paola had to run to catch up with him. Right when Paola's exhaustion was taking over, the thought of not seeing her son again would make her get up and run once again.

By dawn, the Coyote realized something was wrong. He was lost. He did not know where he was or where he needed to go. He thought he was close to the trail he was familiar with, but he did not know which way to go. Paola was just tired, and Hector's fever was lower at that time. The food got wet while crossing the river and the water was almost gone. From that point on, the Coyote told them to ration the water as much as possible.

There was nothing but dirt, rocks, some trees, brush and bushes. Now, the Coyote's pace was slower, and there was no need to rush. They had to keep calm and find a trail. They stopped few times to rest and they walked day and night for the next four consecutive days. They ran out of water by the second day. Hector's fever was coming and going, and with every hour he became more and more lethargic. He cried less and less with no more tears or sweat and even worse, he had stopped urinating. They all were showing clear signs of dehydration, hunger, and exhaustion. Paola had some dry milk in clumps from getting wet but no more water.

Desperation and frustration were once again taking over Paola just as they came across a herd of cattle. The Coyote quickly realized that cows must have water nearby and he was not wrong. They found a tub where the cattle had been drinking, and with little hesitation they all got their hands in the water and cupped a gulp of the greenish, slimy, and smelly water.

The desperation was such that Paola took Hector's empty bottle and filled it up with that water as well. Then she mixed it with some of the dry milk and made something that resembled a bottle of milk. Hector took the bottle and started drinking, but as soon as he could taste the milk, he started crying and turned away from the bottle. Paola tried to convince him to drink but Hector would cry with every gulp. His hunger must have been such that Hector would rather quickly forget the taste of the milk and try again and again as if hoping the taste would be different with every try. The next day, Hector had fever, now with diarrhea and still no urine. Paola knew she was running the risk of losing her son once again.

By the early hours of the fifth day, still under the darkness of the night, they made it to a small town somewhere in Texas. Later that morning, the Coyote found out they were about three hours away from the town where they were supposed to be four days ago. The bad news was they had to walk again. The coyote bought some food, water for everybody and milk for the baby. By now, Hector showed no interest in eating and was even more lethargic.

Paola had to find some kind of medical care but the Coyote refused. By the afternoon of the fifth day, they finally made it to the town where they could get on buses and make it to their destinations. Paola still had to travel to Houston and from there she was supposed to call her brother to pick her up. She did not wait until Houston, though, and called her brother Raul from where she was. Money was wired to her and later that night she finally took a bus to Houston where her brother was waiting for her.

I could not imagine what was going through Paola's mind during those hours in the bus. She did not tell me if she was sleeping or awake. With Hector seriously sick by then, she did not have much time to waste. If she was tired, dirty, hungry, thirsty, upset, frustrated, scared or even sick there was no time to rest, shower, eat, drink, cry or simply let go. Their journey was not over yet.

Hector finally made it to a hospital in Florida on the sixth day. His condition was critical according to doctors. Paola could not tell me his diagnosis or prognosis. All she could say to me was that Hector was hooked to lines with fluids and antibiotics for several days.

It has been 13 years since Paola had to cross the border and she still gets teary-eyed while recounting the story. She was visibly upset and is still, after all these years, fearful of the police and "la migra" (ICE) like the first day she met them. She has been undocumented all these years and has no sign of hope for obtaining any kind of immigration status.

I remember fearing the police and "la migra", and I remember the feeling of uncertainty I carried while being an illegal. I remember not going to the doctor or hospitals because I did not want anybody to find out I did not have a social security number. I remember not being able to go to college because I was not a legal resident of the United States. I remember my mother's job at a mulch factory, and I remember my dad's job cleaning cars and making pizzas. I remember all my limitations, my dreams and my hopes. But see, that's the thing, I remember these things because they are in my past. Now my job is to respond to people's emergencies when they call 911. I am a husband and a father, I continue to go to school, and ten years after I arrived in Florida, I am an American citizen. Life is quite different for Paola.

She still has to deal with the same fears of the first day even though it is thirteen years later. She prefers not to go to the doctor or hospitals. She fears the police. She is constantly looking out for ICE raids. She prays not to be pulled over, lose her job, or even move to a different house.

For Hector, now 14, he feels as American as any other US born citizen. He has never stepped on Mexican soil ever since he almost lost his fragile life 13 years ago. However, he is as illegal as those who crossed the same Rio Grande yesterday. Even worse, we as society will condemn Hector to a life in poverty if he is not allowed to go to college because of his immigration status. Without a higher level of education, Hector will only be able to get a low paying job that requires just a high school diploma.

Paola has been working at the same farm for seven years. Her boss, an older gentleman, has tried to help her obtain an immigration status. The problem is that he has not been able to do anything due to a lack of a legislation that allows undocumented people to lawfully become part of our society. Hector is hopeful that by the time he finishes high school, he can go to college, get a degree, marry his girlfriend, have children, and raise a decent and hard working American family. His hopes and dreams, however, rest on the stroke of a legislator's pen.

For Paola and Hector, being undocumented is not in their past yet. It is a very vivid daily reminder of what they are here in United States, and what they can and cannot do.

The Endless Soul of Immigrants

Being an immigrant means a lot of things,
it means you have left everything behind,
it means you have worked hard,
it means you have an obligation to respect your new land,
it means your heart has split in half
between nostalgia and appreciation,
it means you have taken one of the most
significant steps in your life.
Being an immigrant means you have made some enemies,
but it also means you have made a lot more friends,
it means you are not the first
and probably will not be the last,
it means you are not what you were before,
it means you have changed,
it means you have learned,
it means you have lived
and experience life in a whole different level,
it means you have cried,
it means you have smiled.

Being an immigrant means you have loved
and hated in silence,
it means you never had a chance to say goodbye to some
or give one last hug to others,
it means you feel guilty for not being there
and glad that you left at the same time,
it means you want a chance in life,
it means you want to prove yourself,
it means you are proud of where you came from
and proud of where you are at the same time,
it means you are learning to love again,
it means you are despised by the one that sees you as traitor
and the other one that sees you as an intruder.
it means you are brave, it means you feel weak,
it means you have hope,
it means you have faith,
it means you have dreams,
it means you have what it takes,
it means you miss your loved ones,
But above all, it means you are not alone

CHAPTER TEN

"The land flourished because it was fed from many sources, because it was nourished by so many cultures and traditions and peoples"
— Former President of United States, Lyndon Johnson

While writing the chapter on the myths of immigration, I could not help but think about some of the most relevant facts about American immigration and their importance in any debate. It is very necessary that we all develop an understanding the trends of our immigrant population, their current situation and their possible future outcomes.

American immigration issues are a challenge worthy for the most capable people in our present political world. The solutions have to be well crafted and not half baked. It has to be debated and not argued. That debate has to be thoughtful and not emotional. Only truthful people will find the common ground upon which solutions can take root and grow. Narrow minded individuals are nothing but agitators and distractions that will keep the wise from reaching a place of objectivity and fairness.

Our present immigration challenges are immensely complex because they manage to be both delicate and tough at the same time. They are common sense issues with complicated answers. Their consequences are measurable but their essence is incalculable. American immigration manages to be subjective by nature but objective by definition.

One of the most important reasons why immigration is so complex is that it deals with people and their feelings. Yes, immigration relates to national security, our economy, our laws, and our politics. Yet it also touches our culture, our patriotism, and many aspects of our home lives. In other words, American immigration is directly related to our domestic politics and it affects our social, cultural, and economic policies. It is important geopolitically and it is personal and emotional for everyone that gets involved in the debate.

Because of this, the level of commitment to truthfulness and objectivity found in the privileged people able to lead the changes in our immigration system is of utmost importance. Without it, the immigration debate will be nothing more than a shameful spectacle where all sides of the issue try to demonize the others, where passions take over and the reasoned are overwhelmed by feelings that prevent clear thinking. With that in mind, let's look at a few of the facts of immigration.

Fact I: The Hispanic population living within the United States is growing and is doing so in a faster pace than expected.

This is an inescapable truth in this debate. According to the publication "Poder Hispanic Magazine" (April/May 2011), "Hispanics accounted for most of the growth in every state." Furthermore, "Hispanic population growth is exceeding the census' most recent estimates by more than 4%, amounting to 311,000 more Hispanics in Texas alone." The magazine further shows that the Hispanic population was projected to reach over 50 million by 2012, but the 2010 census numbers show that the actual number of Hispanics in the USA exceeded 50.5 million. Hispanics are 16.3% of the total US population, the fastest growing population in America, the largest minority group, and clearly reached the 50 million mark two years before expected. The Hispanic population grew 46.3% since last census, it accounted for 54% of the overall growth of the total population of United States of America, and without the growth of Latinos in America, the population numbers in some of our states would have actually shrunk.

Population growth is important for two reasons. First, in a country like ours where the middle class traditionally acts as the backbone of our economy, the growth of the middle class guaranties a solid and healthy economy. Businesses flourish due to an increase in demand for supplies, and consumption and spending become great indicators of how fast or slow a country's economy is growing. Classic examples would be the economies of countries like China, India, and Brazil. Their economies are growing not only because of pure numbers but because their middle classes show the biggest leap.

Here in America, the Hispanic population growth rate reached triple digits in some states from the previous census in 2000 to last census in 2010. Some examples are: Mississippi with an increase in Latinos of 105.9%, South Dakota at 102.9%, and Arkansas with 114.2%. Other states like Louisiana showed an increase of 78.7%, Virginia at 91.7%, Oklahoma with 85.2%, Iowa at 83.7%, Washington State hitting 71.2%, and Indiana at 81.7%. (all numbers are from 2010 census according to Poder Hispanic Magazine). Just in my hometown of Port Saint Lucie, the Latino population grew 192% since 2000. It is now 16.6% of the overall population of Saint Lucie County.

The second reason why population growth is important is that growth is essential for our country's labor force. According to Miguel Ferrer, General Manager of AOL Latino, in a report from Huffpost Politics (April 12, 2011), the number of Latinos less than 35 years of age has grown a remarkable 51.5% since 1990. Add to this the 2010 census data showing that among children 17 and younger, Latinos comprise 23.1%. The average age for Latinos in United States is 24 years old compared to the average of 38 years old of the general population in America.

The Hispanic population is younger, vibrant, and an eager part of our society. If allowed to come out of the dark in an organized manner and without disadvantages, it will add to and complement our society. In emerging markets and societies like the Chinese, Indian, and Brazilian, labor forces have played a crucial role in the strengthening of their economies and their relevance in the rest of the world as producer and consumer powers. One can see that China has become a producer power house and its influence can reach almost every corner of our world today.

Fact II: Latinos are showing signs of struggle

Although the Latino population in growing, its success is being jeopardized by our present system, and if it isn't being jeopardized, at the very least it is not allowing Latinos to develop or use their full potential. There are some signs that I believe are reliable indicators of how Latinos are struggling and why it is paramount that we, as a society, correct the current downward trends of our immigrant population.

If we take a look at the origins of our present immigrants, we will find that many are from Latin countries. According to the Urban Institute, in a study by Chaudry and Fortuny called Children of Immigrants and Their Parents: Two Perspectives on Life in America (October 15, 2010), about 42% of all immigrants come from Mexico, another 11% come from Central America and Spanish-Speaking Caribbean, and around 6% comes from South America.

Based on the same study, about 47% of Mexican immigrants have less than high school level of education, another 46% have just high school or some college and only 8% have four year degrees or additional education. At the same time, 20% of East Asian immigrants have less than high school level of education, another 48% have just high school or some college and a much better 32% have four year degrees or more education. As expected, family incomes are directly related to level of education, and for the immigrant families this is not the exception to the rule. The average income for a Mexican family then, is an unsurprising average of around $36,000; in contrast, the average income of an East Asian family is about $86,000.

It is speculated that close to half of Mexican immigrants are undocumented based on a study called Unauthorized Immigrant Population: National and State Trends, published in 2010. According to Jeffrey Passel, senior demographer of the Pew Hispanic Center and D'Vera Cohn, senior writer of the Pew Research Center, about 350,000 children are born each year to at least one undocumented worker. Moreover, an estimated 4 million children have at least one undocumented parent and little over one million children are undocumented themselves. We're not just talking about numbers, though. We're talking about children living among us, living here in our communities today. These children are about 70% more likely to be born in a poor or low income home, which as we all know, hinders anybody's chance of success in our competitive society.

There are some other indicators of how the immigrant population, especially the undocumented one, continues to struggle in our society. For example, according to a Pew Hispanic Center's study Hispanics, High School Dropouts and the GED, only 10% of Hispanic dropouts have a General Educational Development (GED) credential, while at the same time, almost 20% of blacks and 30% of whites obtain their GED, widely regarded as the best second chance pathway to college, vocational training, and military service for adults who do not graduate high school.

The same source also mentions "(Latinos) are much more likely than other American youth to drop out of school and to become teenage parents. They are more likely than white and Asian youths to live in poverty, and they have high levels of exposure to gangs." To be more specific, 26% of Hispanics females are mothers by the age of 19, 17% of Hispanics drop out of high school, and 23% of Hispanics live in poverty.

The urgency of this matter is evident when records indicate that for second generation Hispanic females, the percentage of those who are mothers by the age of 19 drops from 26% to 16%, but increases in third generation females to 21%. I consider this proof that the conditions and circumstances of the environment in which Latinos are being raised is having a very palpable impact on their outcome.

A similar case is shown in the number of Hispanics that drop out of high school. According to the same source, Hispanic dropout rates are 33% for first generation immigrants, it drops to 9% for second generation, but it increases to 12% for third generation. Once again, there is a trend that shows that if the disadvantages of today's Latino population persist in our society, the Hispanic population will not be that young, vibrant, and eager part of our society that is such a source of economic potential and which I so deeply admire.

I want to pause for a moment here and acknowledge that, although there are so many numbers, percentages, statistics and graphics, emotion has a place here and compassion is the most important emotion to indulge in. My first and foremost reason to help others that, like me, are trying to get through their toughest times as immigrants, is compassion. I've included the numbers and the charts for the sake of objectivity and truthfulness. In this book, my intentions have always been to share my recollection of the past along with current facts to gain an understanding of the present and create a better future.

Fact III: Mass deportation isn't a viable option.

A lot has been said about the cost of having undocumented workers, about their effect on wages, and about their burden on society. Not much has been said about the real cost of prosecuting and deporting undocumented workers. However, I found one study that seemed to have legitimate and reputable sources that approached this issue in a serious and non-biased way.

The study, Deporting the Undocumented: A Cost Assessment (Center for American Progress), was authored by Rajeev Goyl, Senior Domestic Policy Analyst and David A. Jaeger, Ph.D., associate professor of economics at the College of William and Mary, conducted the data analysis. This study explores the estimated cost of mass deportation as an option for solving our present situation with immigration. After reading the findings I discovered another fact of American immigration, Mass deportations are financially reckless, are not well perceived by the Latino population, and are not adequate for a nation that promotes the defense of human rights around the world. Humanely speaking, it crosses the line between treating undocumented immigrants as people or treating them as objects.

Proponents of the Arizona Legislation and similar policies that involve the mass deportation of all undocumented immigrants believe that the deterrent effect of such laws and policies would be significant enough to fix the situation—in other words, they hope that the feelings of fear and the harsh living conditions in America would make them go back to their countries of origin or keep them from coming to America in the first place.

It's a Machiavellian way of dealing with our immigrant population and in most cases, even American citizens. According to some estimates, during the Mexican repatriation policy that lasted approximately from 1929 to 1939, over half of the people sent back to Mexico were American citizens less than 18 years of age. These were estimates because the due process that I am so proud of having in our constitution was not given to those repatriated. There was no legislation behind the act, and no executive order signed and therefore, no official records or numbers were kept. Today it is remembered with just some short references in few history books.

Goyl and Jaeger's study divides the cost of deportation of undocumented immigrants into four different factors: Apprehension, Detention, Legal Costs, and Transportation. As a caveat, keep in mind that the study was published in 2005, and it used the numbers, cost figures, and fees from that time period. In 2005, the estimated number of undocumented immigrants was calculated at around 10 million, and the report presumed that the percentage of people leaving voluntarily (if a deportation policy is put in place) would be at around 20%. Now let's examine each of the four factors more closely.

Apprehension is arguably one of the most expensive parts of a mass deportation policy. The report calculated that an agent uses about $ 175,000 per year in resources (between salary, supplies, transportation, and training). It also estimated that about 330 agents were needed to apprehend 3,289 undocumented individuals, deduced from figures pulled from the average of 1999 and 2003. So, based on their calculation, the apprehension of each undocumented immigrant could cost around $17,000. If we use today's numbers of an estimated 12 million undocumented immigrants, minus the 20% that may leave voluntarily (2.4 million), it would leave approximately 9.6 million undocumented for us to apprehend and deport. When multiplied by the $17,000 it would cost to deport them, we come to the conclusion that it will cost the United States of America around $163 billion for the estimated apprehension cost of undocumented immigrants. That doesn't even take into account the increase in costs from 2005 until today.

Detention is another factor to take into consideration, and after seeing the numbers, you will understand why some groups of people (such as the CCA and GEO groups) may be salivating over the potential to profit from our taxpayer money. According to Victor Cerda, acting director of Detention and Removal, United States Department of Homeland Security, in a joint hearing between the Immigration, Border Security and Citizenship, and the Terrorism, Technology, and Homeland Security subcommittees, on April. 14th 2005, the US government only has the resources to hold 19,400 undocumented immigrants. This is yet one more bit of evidence that shows the true intentions of those driving this immigration reform.

The difficulty of finding the real cost of detention for millions of people is due to the differences in cost of living depending on the state and even cities in which the prisons and jails are located. For example, the cost of living in Kentucky is not the same as in California, and services in the city of Miami are considerably more expensive than in my hometown of Port Saint Lucie. However, searching for an average cost, I found that the least expensive figure per inmate was around $60 per day, and the most expensive one was around $130 per day. So, an average of $95 per day could be the cost of housing undocumented immigrants.

Now, at the same meeting I mentioned before between the subcommittees, it was mentioned that on average, each undocumented immigrant spends about 42 days in detention before he or she is finally deported. Obviously, this delay could be addressed by trampling on our own constitution, but at the same time, remember that for-profit prisons are exactly that, for profit, and it may not be convenient for them to expedite deportation processes; in other words, for profit prisons will not complain about keeping an undocumented immigrant an extra couple of days or weeks in their prison.

Let's just say that we start flirting with the line between due process and lawlessness, and we start processing each undocumented immigrant in just two weeks (counting from the moment they get apprehended to the day they get deported). That generates costs for 14 days at $95 per day, multiplied by 9.6 million people. That gives us the amount of $12.7 billion for the estimated detention cost for all undocumented immigrants during a blanket deportation process. Wouldn't it be interesting to find the exact costs of running those prisons so we could see exactly how much the companies stand to gain by pushing for sweeping deportations? Chances are that its quite a lot.

Yet another factor is legal fees and cost of the judicial system. Immigration litigation is typically administered at an immigration courtroom and by an immigration judge. According to the office of The Chief Immigration Judge, Executive Office for Immigration Review, United States Department of Justice (available at *http://www.usdoj.gov/eoir/ocijinfo.htm*), there are about 200 immigration judges that currently hear cases in immigration courts throughout the country. These courtrooms are administered by the Executive Office of Immigration Review (EOIR), an agency within the Department of Justice. For the fiscal year of 2004, the budget for the EOIR was $195 million; that same year, the EOIR processed 163,857 deportations. That gives us an estimated cost of $1,190 per deportation process, which multiplied by the 9.6 million undocumented immigrants, gives us the sum of $11.4 billion for the estimated legal cost of this whole mass deportation policy.

One last important factor in assessing the cost of mass deportation of undocumented immigrants is transportation. After being arrested, detained, and processed, undocumented workers still have to be transported to their country of origin. According to immigration's official website (*http://www.uscis.gov/graphics/shared/statistics/publications/Ill_Report_12 11.pdf*) the most common home country for undocumented immigrant is without a doubt Mexico, with El Salvador and Guatemala coming in as second and third respectively. It is also challenging to find the lowest available air fares online because in most cases, the price of a flight ticket depends on the season and the urgency of the date of the flight. So, based on the estimated time undocumented immigrants could be deported (14 days total), I was able to find the lowest prices online and came up with some numbers. For example, the lowest price of a one-way flight to Mexico is $215, El Salvador $538, Honduras $478, Guatemala $221, Nicaragua $344, Colombia $278, Venezuela $371.

On average, a plane ticket is about $350. This is just a small snapshot of what could be cost the air transportation for undocumented immigrants. Anybody that travels regularly could agree that these prices are rather low at this time and that they could change from one day to another. Using that figure of $350 per plane ticket and multiplying it by 9.6 million people gives us the sum of $3.4 billion for the estimated transportation cost of such mass deportation policy. That total might be lower if we were able to use military flights, but cost analysis isn't available and the political implications would be much more difficult to navigate.

If you've managed to stay with me through all that math, kudos to you! In any case, just stay with me for the final figure… adding the four major factors in estimating the cost of a mass deportation program for 9.6 million souls: $163 billion for apprehension, $12.7 billion for detention $11.4 billion for legal costs and $3.4 billion for transportation, gives us a total operation cost of $190.5 billion.

The numbers are truly staggering. When I began writing this book, I had a rough idea of what I was going to find (or at least that's what I thought I'd find); I would have never imagined that my findings were going to shock me the way they did. Those who say that our immigration challenge is going to be solved with enforcement are not well informed of the implications of such policy—they are trying desperately to mislead us and will continue to push their agenda as much as they can. That's because their agenda is not a solution to our immigration challenge and they know it. No, it is only a solution for those who patiently wait to profit from an endless immigration challenge and those that are consumed by the cancer of prejudice, hatred, and racism.

We need solutions which are designed to enhance the hard working and reasonable middle class that uses common sense to solve problems. A solution from those who have not been cursed by greed, perhaps those in the lower class of America's economy that struggles to remain afloat or those in the upper class that care about their social responsibilities. I can only hope that this book reaches the teachers and students, the mothers and fathers, the colleges and universities, the hospitals and clinics, the nonprofits, the artistic and the scientific, the pragmatist and the dreamers, the citizens and immigrants, the old and young, who are willing to listen with an open mind and contribute to a serious discussion motivated by knowledge and compassion rather than greed.

Fact IV: Undocumented immigrants generate revenue for the United States.

I have a challenge for you. Take any amount of money, it doesn't matter how much. It could be $20 or $1 million. Now take that money and tell me the only thing you could do to keep that money from "Uncle Sam". Sure, you could hide it under your mattress, but what good would the money be then? Now try to invest it in yourself by purchasing real estate, opening a retirement account, buying clothing, groceries, home repairs, anything. Now I ask you, could you really keep it all from Uncle Sam? Is Uncle Sam really your uncle? Sometimes he can appear more like a stalker as he follows you, hand out, demanding the constant toll for our way of life.

We live in a system that moves and grows based on its capacity to promote spending and to collect tax revenues. If you live in America, you know exactly what I am talking about. I ask you now… Do you really think undocumented immigrants have the power to stay clear of paying taxes? Some corporations know the loopholes that keep them away from Uncle Sam's pockets, but, do you know those loopholes? Do you think undocumented immigrants know them?

The fact is, undocumented immigrants create revenue for our government just as we do. The Institute for Taxation and Economic Policy (ITEP) published an article by the Immigration Policy Center of the American Immigration Council titled Unauthorized immigrants pay taxes too,. The article estimated that the state and local taxes paid in 2010 by households that are headed by undocumented immigrants generated collectively over $11 billion that included $1.2 billion in personal income taxes, $1.6 billion in property taxes, and $8.4 billion in sale taxes. The link for the web site is:
http://www.immigrationpolicy.org/just-facts/unauthorized-immigrants-pay-taxes-too

Another article titled Comprehensive immigration reform will create new taxpayers, raise new revenue, cut enforcement costs, and help our economy get back on its feet, by America's Voice, shows that estimates from the Congressional Budget Office (CBO) and the Joint Committee on Taxation, the 2006 Senate bill on immigration, would have raised $66 billion in new revenue over a ten-year period.

A similar analysis from the CBO conducted in 2007 showed that the 2007 senate bill on immigration, would have generated about $48 billion in revenue between 2008 and 2017 as well.

From the same article we learn that the CBO concluded that mandatory E-Verify (a computer data-base that is used to verify immigrant's identity) would decrease federal revenues by $17.3 billion between 2009 and 2018. It also shows that, according to the Perryman Group, deporting undocumented workers would represent a loss of $1.8 trillion in annual spending and $651.5 billion in annual output. Yes, you read that correctly—one point eight trillion dollars in annual spending.

The Immigration Policy Center and the Center for American Progress found that legislation that includes a legalization program for undocumented immigrants would increase U.S gross domestic product (GDP) by at least $1.5 trillion over 10 years. The report also found that the higher earning power of legalized immigrant workers would result in increased tax revenues of $4.5 billion in just three years and that mass deportation would reduce U.S GDP by 1.46% or $2.6 trillion over 10 years.

An additional study by Manuel Pastor of the University of Southern California for The Center for the Study of Immigrant Integration (CSII), found a potential increase of $350 million in tax revenue for the state of California in the short run. California, a state that is in dire need due to budget shortfalls, could find some of the answers to its financial problems on the backs of the immigrants that have given so much to that state already. Once again I encourage everyone to investigate and corroborate this information; there is nothing more valuable than an informed mind. The link for the website is: *http://www.Americasvoiceonline.org/facts/facts-content/good_for_taxpayers.*

CHAPTER ELEVEN

"I SUPPORTED THIS BILL. I BELIEVE IN THE IDEA OF AMNESTY FOR THOSE WHO HAVE PUT DOWN ROOTS AND WHO HAVE LIVED HERE EVEN THOUGH SOMETIME BACK THEY MAY HAVE ENTERED ILLEGALLY."
— RONALD REGAN

The Fair Community Integration Act is my proposed solution to our immigration problems. Its simply a dream, my alternative to the mediocre, money driven, persecution handbook and harassment tool that is the State of Arizona's Senate Bill 1070. My FCI Act is not a law that has been proposed or debated in any kind of legislature; it is merely my personal collection of thoughts and ideas for a more just and effective law.

There are several reasons why I believe opposing the Arizona Law is just not enough. I believe people that have a different point of view or perspective on an issue should present an alternate solution in order to be more credible. Moreover, it is the only way that two opposing sides can negotiate a realistic solution. Without an alternative to the law in Arizona, there is no debate, and without a debate there is only a winner and loser. The immigration challenge that now belongs to our generation does not need a winner or a loser. It needs the best possible solution, for the sake of our community, the well-being of our families, a solution that will keep future generations away from the cancer of racism and strengthen our middle class, our economy, our society, and our country as a whole.

Our American history has shown us time and time again that with every challenging issue and time period comes a vibrant and renewed generation of immigrants; immigrants that enrich our culture and put us once again ahead of other nations. The United States is one of the few countries in the world that has the luxury of having American citizens in and from every single corner of the world. That is synonymous with civilization, freedom, developed societies, innovations, advanced generations, democracy, justice, and the very same values that we so passionately defend and protect in our constitution. These are the same values that not only we in America are proud of, but many others admire.

My FCI Act is intended to be a federal law that will help secure our Mexican-American border, prevent human trafficking, create an adequate and effective immigration policy and finally, promote the fair and necessary integration of undocumented immigrants to our society. My bill proposal has four main components. The first has to do with border security and the need of a larger presence of the Department of Homeland Security. The second has to do with the creation of an effective immigration program, one that encourages legal immigration, aimed to prospective workers willing to perform jobs that companies have not been able to fill in the United States. The third component is the fair and voluntary integration of undocumented workers into our society. An integration that will keep us from allowing the creation of second class citizens. Finally the last component is the Law Enforcement, in which those who remain undocumented in United States, even after the implementation of the FCI Act, will have to be repatriated. Read on to learn more.

Border Security

Securing our borders is easier said than done but definitely necessary. Our borders with Mexico are vast and there are far more dangerous operations running there than the constant flow of immigrants willing to work and become an important part of the labor force of America. I believe that the real threats to our homeland security are the trafficking of drugs, weapon and people across our borders. Drug trafficking is a very lucrative business that plagues our societies, threatens our children and undermine our health.

Drug and gun trafficking are largely responsible for the creation of gangs, bloodshed, and violence in some of our communities. Human trafficking is the systematic abuse, harassment, and violation of human rights in today's world. As American citizens, we have to recognize the real threats and consequences of an unsafe border, with facts and as much objectivity as possible, without half truths or subjectivity.

The biggest challenge of any immigration debate is trying to sort between the friend and the foe, between the real reporting of facts inside a newspaper aimed to inform us, and the phony personal opinions of a talk show aimed to mislead us. When different sides concentrate on just the expression of their emotions, honesty becomes relative and finding the truth in the murky waters of politics will prove to be nearly impossible. A person's biggest challenge in life is mastering the art of honesty. There are some that are very aware of how powerful patriotism is for all of us, and how effective it could be when used to push a personal agenda. Just as patriotism is used against us, so is fear, ignorance, misconceptions, divisions, intimidation, and the distortion of the information.

If the biggest enemies to our communities are drugs, gangs, organized crime, and gun trafficking, then let's go after them. Let's make it hard for clandestine operations to stay in business and freely cross our borders. In my opinion, Juan "the yard guy" and Maria "the housekeeper" do not promote violence in our communities, nor are they in any way the threat that many portray them to be. I believe that continuing to have an undocumented Juan or Maria in our country makes it harder to determine who is here to add to our society, who is here for the wrong reasons, who is an honest and productive immigrant, and who is the criminal that crossed the border to escape justice.

I may not be an expert in homeland security, nor can I know with precision what resources are available to protect the Mexican-American border, but I do know that having a secured border is in our best interest. While some try to score cheap political points at the expense of our fears, the real threats stay unchecked, free to keep making money and hurting our priceless society.

As you read this book, drugs are being smuggle into United States, children are being kidnapped and sold across the border, women are being abused and raped, and weapons are being sold to gangs and drug cartels. Some people could be drowning in the waters of Rio Grande and ironically, others could be dying under the inclement desert sun without a drop of that water. Which of these is a threat to your family? Which of these victims should we simply ignore?

I do not feel the need to elaborate deeper into safety plans or strategies for public safety, because it would be an insult to the organizations that now perform law enforcement in the border regions. Homeland Security and ICE have no need of my humble opinions in order to continue to do their job—and to do it well, perhaps they will have developed their own solutions which we, as a country, have simply not enacted.

Effective Immigration

I believe that an effective immigration program is one that suits our domestic needs, allows companies to employ workers without causing any overhead expenses, and is accessible to the prospective workers.

Being a successful capitalist state means that we have to go back to being producers and not just consumers. Being strictly consumers make us more vulnerable to other economies in order to maintain our way of life. Without a doubt, immigrants have become an important part of America's labor force. Having an effective and accessible immigration process truly encourages legal immigration in our nation. Our current immigration processes do not reach out to the specific kind of workers needed in American industries such as the food industry, farming, clothing, construction and households services.

Until now, our visa process was aimed at specialized professionals and their areas of expertise. It actually works for those employers that need their talents and for those professionals who can wait and afford the process. For example, Exxon Mobil needs to hire an engineer in petroleum to run a platform in the Gulf of Mexico, so the company first tries to hire locally in the United States and if it does not find a suitable candidate then it looks to foreign sources. After all, these are transnational corporations that are familiar with the use of foreign talents to run their operations. An engineer in petroleum has the means and money to access, navigate, and understand the hiring process of a company like Exxon Mobil, making it ideal for highly skilled professionals to be successful in obtaining work permits, visas, and legal residency in America.

On the other hand, a company like Tropicana may not need the same kind of workers with that level of expertise when hiring ground workers to pick, select, and process their products. Its potential workers may not have the same level of education, and they may not have the money or the ability to understand all the complicated forms and steps that any immigration process requires. It comes down to marketing. Just as a company advertises its product aimed to a certain kind of customers, employers need to aim their staffing needs to the right kind of workers as well.

To start, the creation of a hypothetical "labor visa" will allow workers to come legally to the United States from their home countries. It will establish a path for American citizenship after meeting some requirements which may include: ten years of continuous living in the United States, English speaking abilities, and a good standing with the law.

With the benefits of immigrating to work in America come some restrictions and conditions that every FCI Act applicant has to meet. For the first five years, the labor visa holder will be subject to yearly background checks and will also be required to provide the United States Citizen and Immigration Services (USCIS) proof of employment in order to retain his or her labor visa. In addition, the number of visas will have to be regulated as they are now for skilled workers in order to meet only the demands of America's markets.

The Visas could be renewed while in the United States. The worker will also have to prove the completion of a mandatory English course. After the first five years, the immigrant worker could be eligible to change his or her immigration status, from a visa holder to a legal permanent resident, commonly known as a green card holder. Once a permanent resident, he or she will have to take the same steps as any other green card holder in order to become an American citizen, including a period of five years before he or she can apply for citizenship.

Another condition is that during the first five years while they are visa holders, all workers benefiting from this new program will not be able to receive any form of federal, state, or local aid or welfare such as unemployment, food stamps or living expenses. Help from the public sector like FEMA in cases of natural disasters or catastrophes will be allowed as well as federal or state financial aid for school or health.

I firmly believe that properly regulating the numbers of visas, the quality of workers, and creating a program that is accessible to prospective workers while providing a clear and organized set of rules to follow, will without a doubt, give the immigration challenge of our generation a true and just solution to the matter.

11.4

Integration of Undocumented Workers

The integration of undocumented workers to our society is not only an important part of the FCI Act, but it will be a crucial one for our social and economic future. The way I understand capitalism is that it is a socio-economic system that works in conjunction with democracy, aimed to promote wealth in a society. I believe capitalism works by encouraging the creation of a free market which allows entrepreneurs to enter the competitive world of business. Its success is measure by the ability of that society to spend and grow. With that being said, the single most important part of a capitalist society is the middle class.

A strong middle class is the fuel that moves our economy. Because of the competitive nature of capitalism, it is paramount that as many people as possible have the same chances of success. With that in mind, and estimating that a total of twelve million undocumented people live in United States, I believe that a fair and orderly integration of undocumented workers is a better approach than the solution the Arizona law offers. The "hope" that persecution and harassment by law enforcement will discourage hard working people from not crossing or from staying within our borders is truthfully rather pitiful. Once again I find myself looking back to our history, trying to understand how a generation or two ago our society did not provide the same chances of success for all, and how we are literally paying for the consequences of our actions in today's communities.

I do not want to condemn future generations of Americans to a life in poverty, to live in underprivileged communities and to attend mediocre schools. Especially for those who claim to be fiscally responsible and worry about people living off the handouts of the government, it is in our best interest to strengthen today's middle class, adding people to our way of life and making sure future generations are capable of competing in this free market society. Twelve million people cannot be deported without social and financial implications to our daily lives—almost all of which will affect the middle class. That is why a bill that only focuses its attention on law enforcement and does not offer any other alternative or solution has little to no effect in solving our immigration challenge. My FCI Act will allow undocumented immigrants to gain immigration status as long as they meet a certain criteria and maintain a good standing in our communities especially while going through the process of legalization.

First, we need to determine eligibility. It is important to recognize that most of the undocumented workers in our communities are just that... workers. Most of them are currently employed and have a steady source of income. So the first group of undocumented workers that will be able to start their process will be the 'ones that can prove they are working. With the passage of my bill, employers will be able to sponsor any number of undocumented workers already employed without generating overhead expenses. In fact, an employer that is aware of the immigration status of its workers and is willing to sponsor them, will receive a tax break for its efforts in supporting the new FCI Act. Employers are encouraged but not forced to sponsor any undocumented worker. The cost of the tax break given to employers will be offset by the penalties that the undocumented workers will have to pay in order to start his or her immigration process. Moreover, with the FCI Act the employer will be given an additional period of six months to a year, in which the employer can also sponsor newly hired workers and receive the tax break benefits of the law.

Another alternative is the creation of new businesses, in other words, any undocumented worker that has his or her own business and is willing to gain immigration status will have to be registered and/or licensed by his or her company, allowing the company to act as the sponsor of the owner and any other company employee. In this case, a company that acts as sponsor of its own owner will be prohibited from getting any tax breaks for supporting the new law. For example, if an undocumented immigrant is self-employed he or she will have the chance to use his or her company as a sponsor for himself and any other employee, but will not get any tax breaks as written in the law. For those unemployed and undocumented workers not self-employed, they are encouraged to start a new business that will serve as the sponsor needed to start the legalization process.

Of course, there are those who are not employed or self-employed nor do they have the skills to start new businesses. They could be sponsored by direct family members that are employed, self-employed and/or starting new businesses. Military service will be considered an alternative for those seeking to serve our country and gain immigration status. Their immigration status will depend on the successful completion of basic training in any of the branches of the U.S Armed Forces.

College registration will also be considered an alternative for those seeking to be a productive part of our societies as long as they work in United States after completing their degrees. Their immigration status will depend on the successful completion of any two year or higher degree in any college or university of his or her choosing. In-state tuition rates will apply for those who qualify.

Undocumented minors will have the opportunity to gain immigration status as long as they are registered in the school system and their immigration status will also depend on the completion of their high school education.

It is important to mention that just as the FCI Act has specific requirements, rules, and regulations for those who apply for labor visas, undocumented workers here in America will have to comply and meet the same criteria of those applying from abroad in order to successfully complete or even start their legalization processes.

There will be a fee that symbolizes the penalty that will be paid by the undocumented worker in order to offset any cost created by the process of legalization and the absolution of the criminal offense of being undocumented in United States. On top of the penalty, the undocumented worker will be subject to yearly background checks that could keep certain offenders away from legalization. There is the verification of employment, college registration, military service or any other alternative he or she chooses to gain immigration status. Their legalization process depends on the ability of the undocumented immigrant to maintain and successfully complete the listed established goals.

Moreover, the undocumented immigrant seeking immigration status does not qualify for any federal, state or local agency aid or welfare such as unemployment, food stamps, living assistance, etc, while in the first five years of the process or as long as it takes for the immigrant to obtain his or her permanent resident status. Help from FEMA in cases of natural disasters like hurricanes will be allowed as well as federal or state financial aid for school and other vocational careers.

There is also the requirement to register and complete a minimum of ten levels of a mandatory English course that could be similar to the one I completed in Venezuela in order to learn the English language. Note that the only reason I advocate for an English course similar to the one I completed in Venezuela is because I am a living testimony to the success of that specific course.

This English course comes from the University of Carabobo Foundation, a well know public university in Venezuela with a long history of producing high quality English speaking people. The course has ten levels known as "books". Every level is completed in a month, and by the end of "Book 10" there is a diploma that recognizes the completion of the course by the student. This type of course would be ideal for immigrants from all backgrounds and levels of experience.

Law Enforcement

Only after securing our borders, the creation of a new and accessible effective immigration program, and the integration of undocumented immigrants to our communities comes the last and most controversial component of the law. This aspect of the FCI Act, although controversial, is necessary to protect our communities from those who want to remain undocumented in order to avoid domestic or foreign justice.

I feel somewhat comfortable stating that the majority of those who would remain undocumented after being given the opportunity to gain immigration status would do it precisely because they have something to hide and because they would not want to be exposed to a background check. Those are the individuals who are the real threats to the well-being of our loved ones in our communities.

I do not necessarily disagree that law enforcement has to be a component of the solution to our immigration challenge, but what I disagree with is the notion that only law enforcement will be the solution to the complexity of American immigration. Perhaps this is because, as a parent, I feel that if I allow a certain behavior by my children in my house, I cannot later enforce penalties for the same behaviors without losing some legitimacy in my argument, especially if I have neglected or ignored behavior for years. The concept is simple. If a policy or approach to a situation is not effective in solving a problem, I should expect to lose credibility in the eyes of those affected by it. For example, if I ignore or neglect to enforce a non-smoking environment at home, either by allowing my teenager children to smoke or by smoking myself in the house, I cannot penalize my children for lighting up a cigarette while at home without losing credibility in my argument in the eyes of my family.

The law enforcement component of the FCI Act could in actuality be similar to the one proposed by the Arizona legislation, minus the portion allowing racial profiling, harassment, and persecution towards a specific demographic group in our country. Moreover, I believe that by allowing undocumented people to better contribute to our society, our immigration enforcement agencies would not be so overwhelmed as they are today. Immigration and Customs Enforcement would not have to deal with honest and productive American companies; but instead, they could concentrate on protecting our communities from the real threats generated by human trafficking, drug smugglers, and gun trafficking.

The Illegal Immigration Reform and Immigrant Responsibility Act of 1996 established under the prevision 287(g), that The State Department could enter agreements with states and local agencies to perform immigration law enforcement functions. This is when it gets tricky. According to the act of congress in 1996, The State Department's Secretary could request the help of local agencies to help ICE with immigration enforcement duties, but according to the Immigration Act of 1924, the responsibility of the American immigration process is "only" in the hands of the State Department and the Immigration and Naturalization Services.

This is why I firmly believe that the immigration challenge that we face today in our society has to be solved at the federal level. Without the intervention of Congress, the laws of state levels will be continually challenged for their unconstitutionality. The Arizona Law is one example of this. Due to the existence of federal laws and the fact that the responsibility of the creation and enforcement of those laws rest in the hands of federal agencies, state level approaches could be deemed unconstitutional. I can respect the hard work that corporate lawyers and lobbyists put into drafting a law like the Arizona Law. I can even respect their intentions behind such law, but I still find myself questioning both their methods and their motives.

ICE, although controversial at times, has all the power needed to effectively do their job. State laws like the Arizona Law do not add anything new to law enforcement agencies. It does not improve the work of federal agents and in many cases, it just interferes with local law enforcement strategies. This can be seen in the state of Florida where, according to an article published by Scripps Treasure Coast on TCPalm.com, Treasure Coast Sheriffs in Martin, Saint Lucie and Indian River Counties said they were having problems with the proposed immigration bill.

According to the sheriffs, enforcing an "Arizona-style" immigration bill in Florida would require money staff time they did not have a budget for, and it could cause crime to increase as immigrants (legal or undocumented alike) would be more likely not to report crimes. A perfect example of this is found in Martin County, Florida, which has a strong Guatemalan immigrant population. Deputies worked hard over the years to gain their trust and Martin County's Sheriff Crowder said he does not want people to be afraid to report crimes for fear they would be deported. The reality is (I was there once), that immigrants fear law enforcement, regardless of the true existence of a law or not. In other words, my fear of getting in trouble with the law was even more palpable in my times of being undocumented. That fear lives within every undocumented immigrant in America. Undocumented immigrants have fear of everything. Undocumented immigrants are even afraid of going to the emergency rooms. Everywhere you go, a social security number is needed, from filling a job application to getting your water connected at home and even to register in college.

When I was undocumented I feared the police, I feared security guards, I feared the same firefighters that I now form part of. In case this point hasn't already been made clear enough, we do not need the Arizona Law to scare undocumented people away because undocumented people already believe in the existence of such laws.

I have seen badly injured Latinos refusing emergency medical care on the side of the road after a car accident just because they fear me, as an authority figure, and the chances of me finding out that they do not have a social security number. That is why I can understand sheriffs like Mr. Crowder when he said that immigrants will not report crime for the fear of being deported. That is also the reason why I believe the studies that say that undocumented immigrants are less likely to commit crimes or get in trouble with the law, because of the great fear of being deported, because of fear and the shame of letting others know that they are here undocumented, and in some cases, because of the fear of leaving their families and children behind.

The law enforcement aspect of the Arizona Law or any other like it, does not really bring anything new as far as public safety. The tactics and procedures that Arizona-style legislation requires local law enforcement agencies to use are currently being used by federal agencies like ICE— the difference is that ICE does not need to gain the trust of civilians like local police departments do. Federal agencies come, do their job and leave. Local agencies do not have that luxury. They have to work and remain working in those same communities where they performed immigration raids and busts. Their relationships within their communities are based on mutual respect, the trust of the community on the integrity and professionalism of its police, and the cooperation that those agencies get from the communities.

I believe any law enforcement agent would agree with the statement that "it is very challenging to work with communities that do not cooperate with them in solving crimes".

The way federal immigration agencies work has been known to be tough and in some extreme cases inhumane. Once apprehended, undocumented people do not have time to make arrangements for their loved ones, and they are frequently denied of the right to make a phone call. There have been reports of federal agencies like ICE creating fake Occupational Safety and Health Administration (OSHA) training in companies known to have undocumented workers, and apprehend undocumented workers as soon as they show up for their training. They also stalk streets and corners known to be places where immigrants could be found. There have even been reports of ICE agents going to local schools to find out about parent's whereabouts, and intimidating innocent children and exposing them to the rejection of their peers. This is clearly not a job nor the image that any local police departments would want to have in our communities.

There is no easy answer to our immigration situation. It requires tough decisions, commitment, honesty, objectivity, and hard work. Then and only then will we come close to a more effective and realistic solution. Our immigrants are not asking for an easy way out—they certainly didn't need an easy way here—but they do need the possibility of an in, a way to become a citizen. Immigrants don't expect a free pass, they are prepared for a worthy process because they want to feel worthy. Immigrants don't want an empty dream, they want to fulfill the dreams they had when risking their lives to arrive in the United States; like every immigrant to set foot on our soil before them, all they want is the American Dream.

We could pass mediocre immigration laws and speculate about the future of American immigration, or we could adopt a more objective approach, give our immigrants the same opportunity that I was given, and expect with certainty the best results for our communities. Which one do you think will give our country the most prosperous future possible?

CLOSING STATEMENT

In this book, I believe I have given the reader a unique look at our immigration situation and a different perspective to some of the issues that we as Americans are being asked to face in our present time. American immigration is complex and simple at the same time, hard but easy, black, white and everything in between. It is a situation that requires the will of political parties, the vision of leaders, the force of the people, and the passion for defending life that has always characterized us.

I am very aware of all my limitations as a writer, the implications of the decision to make my personal story public, and the fact that, for some time, I have lived in the same darkness and the legal limbo of undocumented people.

However, in this book, I have given you, the reader, an inside look at some of the stories of American immigrants, including my own. I have provided factual information about the immigration process in America and I have exposed the non-factual information about our immigrants and our immigration. I have given you the reasons why I believe the Arizona Law or any other law like it, are actually worthless attempts that only benefit special interest groups and their idiotic approach is an insult to our intelligence. Last but not least, I have presented the Fair Community Integration Act as my proposed law to effectively solve our immigration challenge.

I refuse to think that America is not prepared to solve any challenges including our immigration system. I consider myself an optimist that believes in the immense potential of this great nation, and the common sense that always resurfaces in our society. Our present times require the utmost objectivity and the crafting of effective policies that can realistically promote our common welfare. In other words, to make smart and real decisions to improve our communities and to strengthen our middle class.

Legalizing undocumented immigrants will not be a signal that our doors are wide open for anyone to come. It will mean that we have found the best, humane, and financially sound answer to our particular situation. As long as we create an immigration policy that encourages and reaches the real workers that our economy needs, and not the current immigration system that is sometimes used as a tool to outsource good American jobs, we will have the human capital that our markets need, and the labor force to compete within this global economy.

We have a capitalist system that when used to promote and benefit the middle class, works at its best. When is used to profit special interest groups, it promotes the shifting of wealth that just benefits a few and affects negatively the vast majority of middle class Americans. Beware of the speeches of cheap politicians that try to make you believe that America is a lost, doomed, ruined, hopeless, and weak. Those are speeches created to scare, mislead, confuse, and to use misinformation to benefit only the "few".

America's economy, America's neighborhoods, America's culture, America's society, America's democracy, and the American Dream will always benefit and prevail thanks to legislation that defends and protect Americans. If we take away the politics and exclude the special interest groups from the equations of our lives, we will find that the answers and solutions to our challenges are based on common sense approaches, compromises, and understandings of each other. That is why I believe special interest groups should always be used by "we the people" as tools to achieve our prosperity and nothing more. We are a nation of pioneers, entrepreneurs, innovators, hard workers, dreamers, committed, compassionate, and disciplined citizens who have defended the just and the good against those who are loathsome, hateful and greedy.

We are the same Americans that started the revolution not just to be free from the British crown but to have our own identity. We are the same Americans that gave our own blood to come together as one country, and the same Americans that fought across Europe to defend innocent men, women and children from the oppression of wicked tyrants. We are the same Americans who were able to distinguish the difference between the fairness of an equal society and the repugnant notion of slavery. We are the same Americans that have inspired so many other nations to seek their freedom and liberty. We are the same Americans that value our founding fathers' phrases: "all people are created equal" and "we the people". We are the same Americans I knew while growing up, and the same Americans I see helping each other after hurricanes, floods, tornadoes, earthquakes, fires, and anything, natural or man-made, that threatens not only our own communities but any other in desperate need of a helping hand. That is the America I want my children and grandchildren to grow up in. That is the America I want the rest of the world to know, and the same America I chose September 27th of 2000 to start my new life.

SPECIAL THANKS

First, I would like to thank the miracle I call Life, for keeping its promise and giving me the experiences I need to be able to see and learn more about myself.

My Editor and dear friend Tamara Sockol, her professionalism and hard work were instrumental for the completion of this project.

Thanks again to my mentors Professor Ray Garcia and Dee Ann DuBois for their encouragement and extraordinary dedication to teaching and helping others.

Thanks to all my brothers and sisters at work, for their friendship, guidance, courage, will to serve together, and for making my job "the best damn job in the world". To the dedicated Fire Department that gave me and continues to give me the opportunity to professionally serve my community.

Finally, thanks to all journalists, freelancers, and activists that wrote, spoke, and investigated our immigration situation and made it public, and for their example of dedication and respect for ethical reporting, and for seeking a more just and truthful society.

Thank you for reading! To learn more about the author, please visit *http://www.jgmonaco.com*. If you or someone you know is an immigrant, we invite you to visit *http://www.iusedtobeanillegal.com* and share your own personal story with the community.

www.ingramcontent.com/pod-product-compliance
Lightning Source LLC
Chambersburg PA
CBHW070656290526
45790CB00001B/347